The Oldest Paint Shops in Massachusetts

A PAPER

¶ Read at the Nineteenth Annual Convention of the Society of Master House Painters and Decorators of Massachusetts, held in the American House, Boston, January 13, 1910

By

WILLIAM E. WALL

PUBLISHED BY

WILLIAM E. WALL, SOMERVILLE, MASS.

PRICE 25 CENTS

GRIFFITH-STILLINGS PRESS
BOSTON, MASS., U.S.A.

THE OLDEST PAINT SHOPS IN MASSACHUSETTS

By WILLIAM E. WALL

Mr. President and Gentlemen of the Convention:

In preparing a paper with this title I find it necessary to divide the subject into the oldest paint shops with a continuous existence and oldest paint shops whose existence has ceased, and whose founders have gone the way of all flesh.

The writer does not presume to give the names of all the oldest firms in the State, nor is he positive of the accuracy of all the statements made, as many of the records are furnished by others, and have not been verified by reference to any historical document, yet in the main the statements made are true.

The work of collecting information was begun eighteen months ago. Master painters of every city in the Commonwealth and many of the larger towns have been asked to furnish information on this subject, and a stamped envelope sent for reply. Many have responded, but many others have failed to do so, and in many cases the information has been obtained only by a visit to the master painters or to the public libraries of the older cities.

To keep this paper within reasonable limits, it will be impossible to refer to shops, or firms who are successors of shops, established less than thirty years ago.

As cities grow larger in this new land, and the old order of things in the building trades is rapidly changing, it is well to pause awhile and think of the pioneers of house painting and decorating in the larger centers of the country.

It is a difficult task to undertake, and it is almost impossible to obtain the names of the early master painters in the larger cities of our country. The memory of living men is often the only available source of information, and it is not easy to obtain from them any written account of their early acquaintances among master painters.

It is doubtless true that the builders among the early settlers applied their paint without using skilled painters. Later on, house painters were employed to do the painting, and for at least two centuries have followed that calling.

In the early days the painter prepared all his white lead and colors by grinding them by hand, either with the slab and muller, or with the paint mill. These days have happily passed away, and now all sorts and kinds of pigments, from white to black, can be purchased ground in oil, Japan or water to a stiff paste, or even in fluid form ready for immediate use.

This abundance and variety of material has not proved an unalloyed benefit to the modern painter. He is often quite ignorant of the qualities of the pigments he is using, nor does he realize as did the early master painters that certain combinations of pigments spell disaster when exposed to the weather.

The colonies of Virginia and Massachusetts undoubtedly held the first master painters on this continent. The colonial buildings being composed chiefly of wood, required the protective coatings of paint, and doubtless it was composed chiefly if not wholly of white lead thinned with linseed oil. Some of these early buildings are still standing, and paint applied originally, nearly two hundred years ago, still adheres to the exterior of these houses, many coatings of paint having been applied over the original paint.

Especial pains will be taken in this paper to trace as far back as possible the original firms who founded the business, and to show the connection with shops now existing.

SHOPS THAT HAVE CEASED TO DO BUSINESS

SALEM

(Settled in 1628.)

Among the early records of the town of Salem, we find the
following:

> "Mr. Vernin, his accompt:
>> "Nov. 15th, 1637, Paid to Adams for daubing of the meeting
>> house,   `00–12–04`
>> "Paid to John Bushnell towards the glassing of the windows
>> in the meeting house,   `00–15–06`
> "Samuel Archer's account:
>> "Paid to Adams more for daubing the meeting house,
>>   `00-15-06."`

LYNN

(Settled in 1629.)

In preparing a paper on the oldest paint shops in Massachusetts, it might be well to think for a moment of the oldest painters
of our State. These were the Aborigines, the native Indians
of various tribes, who in the summer time came in great numbers
to the seacoast, especially to Lynn and Chelsea beaches, and
after going through the ceremonies of peace, indulged in ath-
letic sports of various sorts.

The earliest history of Lynn tells us that the faces of many
of these natives were painted in colors to indicate their peaceable
intentions.

The early settlers found high mounds of clam shells on old
Chelsea beach, an evidence of years of feasts at this spot.

The first settlers came to Lynn in 1629. The earliest paint
shop in that town of which we have any record was that of
Jacob Chase, which was established previous to 1775 by Jacob

Chase, Sr. This shop was continued by his two sons, Jacob, Jr., and Philip. The first location was on North Common Street, but when the sons became old enough to enter trade, they separated, Jacob starting business on the corner of Broad and Spring Streets. The shop was continued there by his sons and grandsons until some time during the Civil War, when they sold out to Charles A. Rice and Joseph E. Huse, who continued it until 1875, when Mr. Rice retired from the firm and John S. Wright bought out his interest. The latter remained in partnership with Mr. Huse until the spring of 1878, when he bought out Mr. Huse and took in as a partner, Mr. Henry R. Fellows of Hyde Park. This partnership continued until 1880, when his health giving out, Mr. Fellows withdrew his interest, leaving John S. Wright alone. He remained in the same location until the great fire of 1889, when he was burned out. Even the walls of the brick block which he occupied did not remain standing. In 1890 he hired a lot of land (now occupied by the "Hotel Seymour") and built a one-story building (now standing on a lot in Exchange Street). He remained there until the spring of 1891, when he bought a lot on the same street and moved his building upon it. He remained there until 1895, when he again moved it upon a lot next to his and started to build a brick block, which he completed and occupied the following year. He continued there until the fall of 1907, when not finding any one with money enough to buy him out, he sold the stock at a big discount, disposed of the block and ended the business.

In 1832 we find Jacob Chase, painter and glazier, located on Common Street, and also Philip Chase, Jr., also on Common Street. Other painters in 1832 are: Samuel G. Ashton, Essex Street; Jonathan Buffum, painter and glazier, Union Street; Nehemiah Foster, painter, Common Street; William Luscomb, sign and fancy painter, Pearl Street.

In 1840 we find Jacob Chase, 10 North Common Street; Jacob Chase, Jr., 34 Front Street; Philip Chase, 11–12 North Common Street; Samuel G. Ashton, Essex Street; Samuel G. Ashton, Jr., Essex Street, Woodend; William Luscomb, Pearl Street; Benjamin Luscomb, Pearl Street; Samuel Luscomb, Pearl Street.

In 1851 we find Jacob Chase, 60 Broad Street; Philip Chase, Jr., 20 North Common Street; Samuel G. Ashton, 10 Exchange Street; Benjamin and Samuel Luscomb, 99 Union Street.

In 1854 we find Jacob Chase, 60 Broad Street; Philip Chase, Jr., 25 North Common Street; Samuel G. Ashton, 7 Union Street; Benjamin Luscomb, Union, corner Buffum's Court; Samuel Luscomb, Union, corner Buffum's Court.

BOSTON

No history of the painting business of Boston would be complete without some reference to the Boston Stone.

The Boston Stone, which was imported from England about A.D. 1700, by a painter who had a little shop on the site of the present building, is the oldest relic of the painting art in Boston. It is a sphere of stone about twenty-four inches in diameter, and was fitted into a hollow block of stone which would hold about two barrels of paint.

The paint was mixed thick and placed in the stone trough, and the heavy ball of stone was moved backward and forward the length of the trough. The friction against the sides and bottom of the trough ground the paint in a crude manner.

The round stone is now built into the wall of a building on Marshall Street, where it has remained for over a century. It is named in many descriptions of deeds of land, being used by surveyors as a starting point from which to run their lines.

This property was in the possession of the Childs family for many years. The mill ceased to grind in 1737.

The representation of this stone is the trade-mark of the American Painting and Decorating Co., of Boston.

In the records of a meeting of the Selectmen of the Town of Boston, held December 23, 1761, appears this item:

"Henry Robey, glazier, appeared and agreed with the Selectmen to Repair and new sash the windows of the North Writing School at the rate of Four Shillings old ten p. square, the Glass to be 7 by 9. As also to allow 3/ old Ten p. foot for the Glass that may be taken out."

A record of current events in 1772 informs us that "The

Town House has been painted a neat Stone Color." This paint and all previous and subsequent coatings was removed from the bricks last year. Our old State House was formerly the Town House.

In the records of the Selectmen of the Town of Boston for 1799 appear these two items:

"Paid Edwards for Painting, $14.00."

"Paid Edes, Glazier, $8.25."

The Boston Directory for 1848, under the heading "Portrait Painters," contains the name of William A. Wall. He was no relative of mine, so far as I can learn.

At the beginning of the War of the Revolution, in 1775, the Town of Boston contained about 25,000 inhabitants. At the close of the war the inhabitants numbered about 15,000, and when Paul Revere and his friends formed the Massachusetts Charitable Mechanic Association, in 1795, the population of Boston was about 20,000, less than the number now living in any one of her twenty-five wards.

At this time George Washington was President of the United States, and Samuel Adams, Governor of Massachusetts.

The keel of the frigate *Constitution* had that year been laid in Hartt's Shipyard, at the North End, where she was launched in 1797.

On July 4, 1795, Paul Revere laid the Corner Stone of the present State House on Beacon Hill, and Boston began to assume the dignity of a commercial centre, which she has maintained to this day.

The Boston Directory for 1795 states that among other industries there were in the town, thirty distilleries, two breweries, eight sugar houses, and eleven ropewalks.

These facts should be borne in mind, in considering the conditions under which the early paint shops were established.

Within a hundred yards of where we are now assembled, there met in January, 1795, at the "Green Dragon Tavern," located on Union Street, between Hanover Street and Haymarket Square, a body of Master Mechanics, "For the purpose of consulting on measures for petitioning the General Court to revise and amend the law respecting apprentices."

Paul Revere, who acted as Chairman at this and later preliminary meetings, became the first President of what was later designated the Massachusetts Charitable Mechanic Association.

Out of a total of eighty-three signers to the Constitution, three were painters, viz., Samuel Gore, John Cotton, and Samuel Perkins.

Samuel Gore was the first treasurer, being elected at the adjourned meeting of April 16, 1795. He was re-elected for several years. John Cotton and Samuel Perkins were afterwards presidents.

Samuel Gore was born in Boston, February 6, 1751. His father was John Gore, a painter by trade, who, about 1730, kept a shop, and lived in a dwelling house more than fifty years on Court Street, at the head of a narrow passageway, leading from Court Street to Brattle Square, called Gore's Alley. This passageway, now widened, is called Brattle Street.

Samuel, his son, learned the trade of his father, and succeeded him in business at the old stand.

His father was a Tory, and left Boston and went with General Gage to Halifax, N. S., in 1776. His son was a Whig, and was active in all measures opposed to the British Government. He was one of the Boston Tea Party.

He invested a large sum in the establishment of a glass works on Essex Street, which proved a failure, and made him poor. He withdrew from the Association about this time. He died in Boston, November 16, 1831, aged eighty years and nine months. He was an elder brother of Christopher Gore, Governor of Massachusetts.

John Cotton was the eldest of seventeen children of Solomon Cotton. He was born in Boston, June 9, 1775, served a regular apprenticeship to Samuel Gore, and carried on the business of house, ship and sign painting for many years.

By the death of his brother, Edward Cotton, he came into the possession of a bookstore, to which he added an apparatus for printing, and carried on the two branches of the business in connection with another brother and a man by the name of Barnard, at the corner of Washington and Franklin Streets. He served the Massachusetts Charitable Mechanic Association at various times, in the capacity of Secretary, Trustee, Vice-President, President, and Treasurer, and his fellow citizens, as a Representative, Senator, member of the Board of Health, Fire Ward, and member of the Constitutional Convention of 1820.

He was well known as a man of intelligence, sound principles, urbanity of manners, and fidelity of friendship. In early life he made a voyage to Europe. His health was feeble in his later years. He died November 25, 1838, aged sixty-eight years.

Samuel Perkins was born in Boston, September 2, 1770. His father was William Perkins, Major in Colonel Crane's Regiment of Artillery of the Massachusetts Line, in the Revolutionary Army, and after, with the rank of Colonel, was commander of the troops stationed on Castle Island, now Fort Independence.

When thirteen years old, Mr. Perkins went as an apprentice to Maj. John Johnson, a well-known portrait painter, who was located at Court Street, near the head of Gore's Alley.

His object was to learn the common, as well as the ornamental branches of the art. It is not known how long he continued with Johnson, but at the age of nineteen he began the painting business, chiefly on houses and ships, by himself, and continued it until about 1815, when he undertook to paint oilcloth carpets.

This business he continued for some years in Boston, till the increased demand for his work induced him to build a large factory in Roxbury.

He was quite successful until rival manufactories in New York created a competition, which, together with his age, induced him to retire from active pursuit of business.

Paul Revere served four terms as president. He was born in Boston in 1734. His father was a French Huguenot, who spelled his name "Riviore." He was a goldsmith by trade, and his son Paul learned the same trade, at which he became expert, and later became skilful in drawing and engraving.

While young, he enlisted in the Army and became a lieutenant. It is not necessary to refer here to his patriotism. That has been perpetuated in prose and verse, by some of our ablest writers.

He died in 1818, at the age of eighty-four.

Some thirty-five years ago, Mr. A. P. Boyce, a well-known sign painter, while cleaning off the signboard, found the name of Paul Revere on the corner of the sign. It is not impossible that he might have occasionally painted signs for merchants.

MASTER PAINTERS ADMITTED TO THE MASSA-CHUSETTS CHARITABLE MECHANIC ASSOCIATION, 1800 TO 1899

1800. Out of more than one hundred members admitted in 1800, but two were painters, viz., Samuel Hastings and George Vaughn.

1801. In 1801 Michael Roulstone, glazier, and Abraham Edwards and James Henderson, painters, were admitted to membership.

1802–4. None were admitted in 1802, 1803 and 1804.

1805. George Gore, painter, was admitted in 1805.

1806–8. None were admitted in 1806, 1807 or 1808.

1809. In 1809 Henry Tolman and La Fayette Perkins were admitted.

1810–13. None were admitted in 1810, 1811, 1812 or 1813.

1814. In 1814 Jeremiah P. Smith of Roxbury, painter and glazier, was admitted.

1815. In 1815 John Green, Jr., was admitted.

1816–17. None were admitted in 1816 or 1817.

1818. In 1818 sixty-seven were admitted to membership, of which the following were painters: Samuel Perkins, painter; Christopher Gore, painter; James C. R. Bangs, painter; John R. Penniman, artist; Simon Gardner, painter; William Baker, painter; Sewall Goodenough, painter.

In this year a new certificate of membership was designed by John R. Penniman and engraved by Annin & Smith.

1819–21. None were admitted in 1819, 1820 or 1821.

1822. Edward Phillips was admitted in 1822.

1823. None were admitted in 1823. In this year John Cotton was President.

1824. None were admitted in 1824.

1825. In 1825 George Redding and Edward Russell were admitted.

1826. In 1826 Joel Prouty, painter, was admitted.

1827. In 1827 John Parks, painter, was admitted.

1828. In 1828 Dwight Prouty, Francis H. P. Homer and George Yendall, painters, were admitted.

1829. None were admitted in 1829.

1830. In 1830 Southworth Bryant, Charles Henderson and Ebenezer Scott were admitted.

1831. Reuben T. Robinson, Ruel Baker and Charles Redding were admitted in 1831.

1832. In 1832 Isaac Bird, paperhanger, and Albert Homer and Timothy S. Nichols, painters, were admitted.

1833. In 1833 Kimball Gibson, James K. Frothingham of Charlestown, portrait painter, and Horace A. Breed, painter and glazier, were admitted.

1834. In 1834 John Mack and William Dow, painters and glaziers, and Jefferson C. Farrer and William Dove, painters, were admitted.

1835. Cyrus Hastings, Joseph Belcher and Horatio G. Somerby, painters, were admitted in 1835.

1836. George D. Wyman, painter, was admitted in 1836.

1837. In 1837 the following were admitted: Daniel L. Ware, painter; James Snow, painter; Charles A. Smith, painter; Andrew P. Young, painter; Gardner Edmands, painter and glazier; John Bates, painter.

1838. In 1838 none were admitted.

1839. In 1839 Ebenezer H. Hutchings, paper-hanger, was admitted.

1840. In 1840 the following were admitted: Bradley M. Clark, Samuel D. Bates, David Granger, Warren Gill, John Boynton.

1841. Thomas C. Savory, painter, was admitted in 1841.

1842. Joshua Holden was admitted in 1842.

1843. In 1843 Calvin W. Haven was admitted.

1844–46. None were admitted in 1844, 1845 or 1846.

1847. Edward Hemenway, painter, and William Tileston, varnisher and polisher, were admitted in 1847.

1848. In 1848 none were admitted.

1849. In 1849 Benjamin F. Baker, painter, was admitted.

1850. In 1850 William F. Goodwin, painter, was admitted.

1851. None were admitted in 1851.

1852. Simon Hastings was admitted in 1852.

1853.	In 1853 John F. Bates was admitted.

1854.	In 1854 Thomas D. Morris and Edward A. Vose, painters, were admitted.

1855.	None were admitted in 1855.

1856.	In 1856 the following were admitted: Robert Wharton, Benjamin F. Baker, Charles H. Knox, Charles E. Noyes, John Cotton.

1857.	Horace C. Rose was admitted in 1857.

1858.	In 1858 Thomas C. Savory, David B. Webster and Thomas J. Lyford were admitted.

1859.	In 1859 Charles S. Burgess was admitted.

1865.	In 1865 William Carl, fresco painter, was admitted.

1866.	In 1866 Cyrus T. Clark was admitted.

1868.	In 1868 B. W. Wentworth, painter, was admitted.

1869.	In 1869 Eli F. Redman, J. D. Bragdon and H. M. Hutchins were admitted.

1870.	In 1870 John C. Simpson and William L. Barnes were admitted.

1871.	In 1871 James W. Bell and Lucas Haberstroh were admitted.

1872.	In 1872 Thomas H. Winslow and Thomas H. Burgess were admitted.

1873.	In 1873 James R. Putnam, Horace Weston, James H. Thayer and Farwell J. Thayer were admitted.

1874.	In 1874 James I. Wingate was admitted.

1875.	In 1875 Marshall Gordon was admitted.

1878.	In 1878 Albert Haberstroh was admitted.

1879.	In 1879 Charles H. Bell, Thomas S. Hodge and J. H. Boody were admitted.

1880.	In 1880 Edwin P. Longley was admitted.

1881.	In 1881 William G. Whitney, M. F. Shay, William E. Shay and N. G. Finney were admitted.

1882.	In 1882 Henry Paddock, James L. Blackmer, John D. Campbell and J. B. Hand were admitted.

1883.	In 1883 Lewis F. Perry and Robert R. Rose were admitted.

1888.	In 1888 John White, painter, was admitted.

1895.	In 1895 William Lamprell, decorator, and Albert L. Knox, painter, were admitted.

1899.	In 1899 William W. Chapman was admitted.

OBITUARY NOTICES OF MASTER PAINTERS, M.C.M.A.

John Bates. John Bates, painter, familiarly known as "Deacon Bates," was born at Weymouth in 1797. He was admitted to the Massachusetts Charitable Mechanic Association in 1837. He lived on Temple Street and had his shop on Province Street. He died in 1863, aged sixty-six years.

James K. Frothingham. James K. Frothingham was born in Charlestown, Mass., in 1785. He was a carriage, sign and ornamental painter. He joined the Massachusetts Charitable Mechanic Association in 1833 and died in 1864. He was for years in probate, real estate, etc.

Charles Redding. Charles Redding was born in Boston in 1803. He was a house and sign painter, and was in business with his brother on Court Street for nearly forty years. He joined the Massachusetts Charitable Mechanic Association in 1831. He died in 1864, aged sixty-one. He with his brother founded the business of Redding, Baird & Co., dealers in stained glass and makers of ecclesiastical and memorial windows.

Reuben T. Robinson. Reuben T. Robinson was born in Barre, Mass., in 1793. He was a soldier in the War of 1812, and was in company with several well-known painters. He joined the Massachusetts Charitable Mechanic Association in 1835 and died in 1865.

John P. Orcutt. John P. Orcutt was born in Boston in 1809. He served seven years to learn the trade of sign painter. He joined the Massachusetts Charitable Mechanic Association in 1837 and died in 1866, aged fifty-seven.

John Green, Jr. John Green, Jr., was born in Boston in 1789. He learned the painters' trade and had a shop first in Roxbury. He later removed to the South End. He served in the City Council and State Legislature, was engineer in the Fire Department, a member of the Ancient and Honorable Artillery Company, and joined the Massachusetts Charitable Mechanic Association in 1815. He died in 1866, aged seventy-seven. He was known as "Old Johnny Green."

Enoch H. Snelling. Enoch H. Snelling, plumber and glazier, was born in Boston in 1792. He followed glazing as a business. He was a member of the School Committee and the Common Council, also of military organizations. He joined the Massachusetts Charitable Mechanic Association in 1829 and died in 1866, aged seventy-four.

CHARLES A. SMITH. Charles A. Smith was born in Boston in 1814. He was in business in Boston for thirty-three years. He was located at 11 Kingston Street in 1849, and at 36 Kingston Street in 1865. He joined the Massachusetts Charitable Mechanic Association in 1837 and died in 1868, aged fifty-four years.

HORACE C. ROSE. Horace C. Rose was born in Watervliet, N.Y., in 1816, and was a master painter for many years. He joined the Massachusetts Charitable Mechanic Association in 1857. He died in 1873, aged fifty-seven years.

EDWARD A. VOSE. Edward A. Vose was born in Boston about 1824. He was an ardent politician and fluent talker and was once nominated for Governor. He joined the Massachusetts Charitable Mechanic Association in 1854 and died in 1873, aged forty-nine.

WILLIAM F. GOODWIN. William F. Goodwin was born in Bradford, Vt., in 1814. He came to Boston when a young man, having learned the painters' trade. He went into business alone about 1836, and later took E. S. Goodwin as partner. In 1846 they were located at 169 Tremont Street.

William F. Goodwin was a director in the Revere Bank, and President of the Boston Musical Education Society. He served in the city government several years, and joined the Massachusetts Charitable Mechanic Association in 1850. Later he removed to New York, where he organized the "Oratorio Society of New York." He died in 1875, aged sixty-one.

HORATIO G. WALDRON. Horatio G. Waldron was born in Dover, N.H., in 1816 and learned the painters' trade in this city. He joined the Massachusetts Charitable Mechanic Association in 1856 and died in 1876, aged sixty.

BRADLEY M. CLARK. Bradley M. Clark was born in Acworth, N.H., in 1810 and learned the trade of a painter; with three others he formed the firm of B. M. Clark & Co., whose shop in 1846 was located at 71 Broad Street. He joined the Massachusetts Charitable Mechanic Association in 1841. He died in 1876, aged sixty-six.

ELI T. REDMAN. Eli T. Redman was born in Birmingham, England, in 1833. He learned the painters' trade in his native country. He joined the Massachusetts Charitable Mechanic Assocation in 1869. He died in 1876, aged forty-three.

WILLIAM CARL. William Carl was born in Germany in 1831. He learned the trade of fresco painter and decorator, and was in business in Boston till 1871, when he removed to New York, and later to Providence, R. I. He joined the Massachusetts Charitable Mechanic Association in 1865. He died in Providence, R.I., in 1877, aged forty-six.

SAMUEL D. BATES. Samuel D. Bates, painter, joined the Massachusetts Charitable Mechanic Association in 1841. He was in business at 57½ Court Street (Scollay Building) in 1846, and in his later years at 25 Bromfield Street. His residence was on Linwood Street, Roxbury. He died in 1877. His age is not stated.

HORACE A. BREED. Horace A. Breed was born in Lynn, Mass., in 1806. He followed the trade of painter and paper-hanger for years in this city, and later he dealt in paper hangings. He joined the Massachusetts Charitable Mechanic Association in 1833. He died in 1878, aged seventy-two.

ROBERT WHARTON. Robert Wharton was born in Vassalboro, Maine, in 1815. He learned the painters' trade and went into business first in Bangor. He came to Boston and carried on business for forty years. In 1849 he was at 395 Washington Street, under the name of Wharton & Locke. He joined the Massachusetts Charitable Mechanic Association in 1856 and died in 1879.

THOMAS D. MORRIS. Thomas D. Morris was a native of Sumterville, S.C., but came early in life to Boston. He did a large painting business at the West End. Later in life he went into the manufacture of paints. For a while he did well, but failing to protect his specialty by a patent, larger manufacturers supplanted him and seriously crippled his income.

He was admitted to the Massachusetts Charitable Mechanic Association in 1854. He was a member of the Handel and Haydn Society, and served two terms in the Legislature. He was a pronounced anti-slavery man, and a man of sterling integrity. He died in 1881, aged sixty-nine.

CALVIN W. HAVEN. Calvin W. Haven was born in Charlemont, Mass., in 1803. He came to Boston at the age of thirteen, and soon after learned the painters' trade from Asa Bugbee, for whom he worked until he commenced business for himself in 1825. He joined the Massachusetts Charitable Mechanic Association in 1843. Later he was a dealer in paints. He was a member of the Common Council. He died in 1882, aged seventy-nine years.

GEORGE YENDELL. George Yendell was born in Boston in 1805. He was admitted to the Massachusetts Charitable Mechanic Association in 1828, having served his time with Mr. John Cotton, one of the original members of the Massachusetts Charitable Mechanic Association.

In 1832 his place of business was located at 74 Congress Street. In 1850 his shop was at 13 Lindall Street, and in 1865 at 22 Hawley Street. He made a specialty of imitations of wood and marble.

He died in 1882, aged seventy-six.

HIRAM TUCKER. Hiram Tucker was born in Haverhill, N.H., in 1822, son of Nathaniel Tucker, a house painter of Boston. He served his time with his father and began business for himself in Cambridge, Mass., in 1845, remaining until 1848. He was an inventive genius and patented a process for making iron mantelpieces and painting them to represent marble.

He was a brother-in-law of Elias Howe, the inventor of the sewing machine, and the latter was in his employ while perfecting his patent.

Mr. Tucker later invented the spring bed. He manufactured ninety thousand spring beds for the United States Government, for use in hospitals, etc. He patented several other things, such as varnish, extension chandeliers, etc. In 1874 he invented the paint can still used by John W. Masury for colors, also a horse-car switch.

He was admitted to the Massachusetts Charitable Mechanic Association in 1866. He died in 1882, aged sixty.

GEORGE W. SPRAGUE. George W. Sprague was born in Boston in 1823. He was apprenticed to James Hazeltine, painter. In 1844, at the age of twenty-one, he commenced business for himself. For fourteen years his partner was Sylvester Barnard, as Sprague & Barnard. Mr. Sprague was admitted to the Massachusetts Charitable Mechanic Association in 1860.

Mr. Sprague was a member of the Common Council in 1860, 1861, 1862 and 1863, and a member of the Board of Aldermen in 1864 and 1865. He died in 1882, aged fifty-nine.

Sprague & Barnard were in business at 123 Dorchester Avenue, South Boston, called the "Turnpike" before 1850. Mr. Barnard died in 1863, and George Sprague conducted the business until his death. He had no successor in business.

ALBERT HOMER. Albert Homer was born in Boston in 1805. At the age of fourteen he was apprenticed to Daniel Ware, painter, who in 1820 was in business on Cambridge Street.

In 1827, at the age of twenty-two, he commenced business for himself, and continued to do so until his death. He was admitted to the Massachusetts Charitable Mechanic Association in 1832. He died in 1883.

THOMAS H. BURGESS. Thomas H. Burgess was born in Kingston, Mass., in 1829. At the age of seventeen he came to Boston, and served his time to his brother, Chas. S. Burgess, a well-known master painter. Later he was in business on his own account.

He was admitted to the Massachusetts Charitable Mechanic Association in 1872. He died in 1885, aged fifty-five.

WILLIAM L. BARRUS. William L. Barrus was born in Warren, R.I., in 1829. He learned the painters' trade in Providence, R.I., and came to Boston. He was in business on Leverett Street in one shop for over thirty-three years. In 1870, the firm was Barrus & Cassell.

He served in Company A, Twelfth Massachusetts Volunteers, in the war, and was wounded.

He joined the Massachusetts Charitable Mechanic Association in 1870 and died in 1885, aged fifty-six.

GARDNER EDMANDS. Gardner Edmands was born at Framingham, Mass., in 1812. He learned the painting business and came to Boston, and soon started in business for himself. His health failing, he soon gave up business. He joined the Massachusetts Charitable Mechanic Association in 1837. He died in 1886, aged seventy-four.

CHARLES E. NOYES. Charles E. Noyes was born in Newburyport in 1806. His father, Jacob Noyes, came to Boston, where he carried on the business of house painting. His son learned the trade and soon started in business for himself. In 1846 his shop was located at 100 Harrison Avenue. He joined the Massachusetts Charitable Mechanic Association in 1856, and retired from business about 1882. He died in 1887, aged eighty-one.

EDMUND D. CASSELL. Edmund D. Cassell was born in Boston in 1802. He learned the trade of house and sign painter, and after more than thirty years as a master painter he retired from business, about 1876. He joined the Massachusetts Charitable Mechanic Association in 1840. He died in 1888, aged eighty-seven.

JOSEPH D. BRAGDON. Joseph D. Bragdon was born in Kennebunk, Maine, in 1826. He came to Boston as a boy, and learned the trade of a house painter. During the war he served in the Fifth Massachusetts, and later in the Eleventh Massachusetts Battery, to the close of the war.

He lived in Dorchester. His place of business was on Harrison Avenue.

He joined the Massachusetts Charitable Mechanic Association in 1869 and died June 10, 1893, aged sixty-seven.

DAVID C. WESTON. David C. Weston was born in Vermont in 1815, and learned the painters' trade. He lived in Charlestown and was in business over forty years. He joined the Massachusetts Charitable Mechanic Association in 1857. He died in 1893, aged seventy-eight years.

MARSHALL GORDON. Marshall Gordon was born in Fryeburg, Maine, in 1832. He learned the painters' trade and commenced business on his own account in his native town. He carried on business in Boston for over thirty years. In 1885 his shop was at 10 Pleasant Street. He joined the Massachusetts Charitable Mechanic Association in 1875. He died in 1895, aged sixty-three.

THOMAS C. SAVORY. Thomas C. Savory was born in Boston in 1818. He learned the trade of sign and fancy painter, serving seven years. Later he succeeded to the business of his employer and followed it for many years. He joined the Massachusetts Charitable Mechanic Association in 1858. He died in 1896, aged seventy-eight.

SAMUEL HASTINGS. Samuel Hastings was born in Boston in 1825, and learned the painters' trade. He was in business on Charles Street for over thirty years. He joined the Massachusetts Charitable Mechanic Association in 1852. He retired from business about 1890 and died in 1896, aged seventy-one.

WILLIAM H. EMERSON. William H. Emerson was born in Boston in 1827. He served his time to Kimball Gibson, who in 1849 had a shop at 40 Bromfield Street. He opened a shop on Charles Street, where he continued in business for more than twenty years. Later, he removed to Chicago where, in 1892, he was in business on Cottage Grove Avenue. He joined the Massachusetts Charitable Mechanic Association in 1860. He died in 1898, aged seventy-one.

CYRUS T. CLARK. Cyrus T. Clark was one of the most noted painters of Boston in the last generation, as he was a large contractor, and was a very well known character in business circles.

He was born in Malden, Mass., in 1824, and served his time in White's shop on Hanover Street, about 1844, and soon after went into business for himself. In 1849 he was located at 17 Devonshire Street. He formed a partnership with William S. Brazer, the fresco painter, about 1855, but the partnership soon dissolved, and Mr. Clark continued the business in his own name till his death.

About 1857 Mr. Clark bought out the shop of R. T. Robinson, corner Hanover and Richmond Streets, where he remained for many years.

Mr. Clark removed his shop to 45 Wareham Street about 1870, and the business has continued in that location until December, 1909, as the Cyrus T. Clark Co. The firm failed and retired from business in 1909.

Mr. Clark joined the Massachusetts Charitable Mechanic Association in 1866, and was one of the early members of the Boston Master Painters' Association, and the Master Builders' Association. He died in 1899, aged seventy-four years.

THE OLDEST PAINT SHOPS IN MASSACHUSETTS

BOSTON

My friend, Thomas W. Lindsay, writes me as follows:

"I have delayed writing you about what I could tell you about the old paint shops in the South End, because I wanted to talk with an old friend of mine, who was an old man in the shop when I was an apprentice boy, as I knew he could give me some information that might be of use to you. He showed up today, and I wish you could have been here, as you would certainly have obtained some color for your story, even if the facts were rather vague.

"He learned his trade with 'Old Deacon Bates,' who kept his shop on Province Street, I think under the old Montgomery House. He was bound out to Deacon Bates by his father. He lived at the old Deacon's house, as did the other apprentices, although his own home was near by, on Oliver Place. The Deacon kept a strict hand on them, and they had to do the chores around the house after working in the shop, and had to stay in nights. What those boys didn't do to the old man was a caution. One story he tells and I believe it, too. One hot summer day, the old Deacon made him carry a pair of steps that weighed about a ton from the shop on Province Street away up to Chester Park, where they were doing a job. When he got to the job he was so mad that he took them up on the roof, and hove them over into the back yard, smashing them into kindlings.

"When the war broke out, he enlisted, and when the company paraded on the Common the old Deacon made him a present of a pistol. When he came back from the war he worked in several shops, among others, for L. F. Perry, who had his shop then on School Street in the Ticknor Publishing House, having moved his business in from Dedham. Perry had for a foreman then old Paddy Golden, who afterward had a shop on Dedham Street. Another old boss he worked for was 'Old Bill Nye' on Howard Street, who was another character, of whom as many stories are told as the old original 'Cy Clark.' At that time, also, 'Old man Burgess' kept a shop on Hawley Street, and he had a son Tom. Jim Wingate worked there and afterward he and the son Tom started a shop on Tremont Street, near Castle, as Burgess & Wingate, I think. They afterward separated, Burgess keeping the shop and Wingate starting a new one. When Tom Burgess died, his two head men, Walter McCreary and John Noyes, started out down at the West End. They afterward separated. McCreary has since died. Another old shop on Province Street was 'Old Man Martin's.' From this shop Weston & Putnam started out, who have been succeeded by F. M. Rogers. Other shops in the neighborhood were 'Old Man Goodwin's' on Bromfield Street, 'Old Man Hathaway's' on Beach Street, 'Old Man Griffith's' on Avery Street, 'Old Man Green's' on Washington Street, near Mott. Comical, no front names remembered, only 'Old Man,' and they were old men. However unhealthy our trade may be, those men, by clean living, all managed to be able to scratch gray hair.

"My old friend is seventy-two. Haberstroh & Needham was another old shop on Washington Street, near Kneeland, and, of course, you know the number of celebrities who were dug up there — W. E. Norton, William F. Halsall and lots more. (Both Norton and Halsall were later celebrated marine painters.)

"Coming up near Dover Street, there was the only paint shop outside of Scotland — the great William J. McPherson's. A list of the men who have started in business from that shop would include many of our most prominent members, and a history of this shop would make an article of itself and be worthy the pen of a master.

"Modlich, also, whose shop is now on Church Street, at that time had his shop near the Park Street Church. James W. Bell, McPherson's foreman, started a shop in 1869 on Tremont Street, near Paul's Mill, moving his shop the following year to the shop now occupied by Peters & Lindsay. He retired from business in 1875, making his pile in six years. He was succeeded by his brother, Charlie, who on his death, in 1898, was succeeded by the firm of Peters & Lindsay, making this shop forty years old.

"In 1886 Sam Alexander, Bell's foreman, at that time started in business on the corner of Chapman and Tremont Streets, alongside of Campbell's paint shop. They were like twins, and when they had to move they went upon Warren Avenue together. Sam moved from Warren Avenue to Wareham Street, and from there to Dudley Street. Campbell moved from Warren Avenue to 10 Clarendon Street.

"Other old shops in the South End were C. H. Knox's on Springfield Street. From this shop I believe 'Eddy Beck' started out. This shop is now run by D. J. Bryan. Jim Rawson's shop was on Canton Street; when he died his business was continued by Gallagher. Turell's shop was on Brookline Street, near Tremont. McCormack & Poole's shop was on Worcester Street, now carried on by McCormack's son, Frank.

"All these men have wiped their pots down long ago. W. A. Spooner kept a shop on Warren Avenue, near Tremont Street, another fine old man. Tom Callahan kept shop on Dover Street, a real dude, who, when a journeyman, used to come to work with a plug hat and kid gloves. I hope you will find something in this that will be of use to you.

"Yours sincerely,

"T. W. LINDSAY."

Mr. Thomas Shay of Roxbury writes me as follows:

"The oldest painter I know anything about and whom I have seen was a Mr. Perkins of the North End, who had the contract to paint the frigate *Constitution*, when she was built at the North End. Some years after that he started a factory in Roxbury for the manufacture of oil-cloth carpets, in which business he continued till his death. The next oldest painter I knew was named Seaver, who painted and glazed the Universalist Church at the junction of Dudley and Washington Streets, near Shawmut Avenue. He set every light of glass in the building with his own hands. That was in the year 1810.

"The next oldest painter I remember was G. W. Wilson, with shop on what is now called Linden Park Street, in 1839. Some years after he had as partner Brandford S. Ray.

"The next I recall was a man named Wiggin, with three sons, Joe, Frank and George, long since passed away.

"As we walk down Washington Street, then the main street, we come to where the Rockland Bank now stands. Here stood the shop of George B. Davis. It was a paint shop a great many years. He was succeeded by Thomas M. Hodge. When the land was taken to build the bank, he removed to Warren Street, on the land where the shop occupied by Shay Brothers now stands.

"Passing down Washington Street, till we get to Winthrop Place, we find the spot where William Dove carried on the business more years than I can remember.

"On Warren Street for a number of years was located B. F. Ayers. On the corner of Eustis and Albany Streets was the shop of Charles Erskine, who carried on the business there a number of years, and was succeeded by Palfrey & Agnew. After William Agnew's death, the shop was continued by his son George.

"I hope you will be pleased with these few lines, and that I have understood what you desired me to say."

Mr. James Harrison of Stoneham writes me as follows:

"I received a letter from you, asking for a little information on the old paint shops. I remember these old shops, dating from 1858.

"Paint shops on Cambridge Street, or the streets running off Cambridge Street: I. Balcolm, Russell Street; John Rolland, Blossom Street; Longley Brothers, Cambridge Street; David C. Nye, Howard Street Court; John Magee, Leverett Street.

"In Scollay Square, there was on Tremont Row, W. J. McPherson, near the corner of Pemberton Square. He kept upstairs. Then he moved to a store opposite the old Museum on Tremont Street, afterwards to a shop on Tremont Street, afterwards occupied by L. F. Perry.

"In Scollay Square there was an old triangular building that divided Court and Tremont Streets, in which was the paint shop of Samuel Bates, in the second story.

"Down Hanover Street, corner of Richmond Street, there was a shop kept by Mr. White (brother-in-law of D. C. Nye). In White's shop Cyrus Clark served his time. Then Clark & Brazier afterwards ran this shop, or some shop nearby. Mr White moved to Melrose and did business there for some time. I remember him well. He died over twenty years ago.

"Near the old National Theatre on Merrimack Street, there used to be a paint shop in which Thomas Huntoon served his time. Huntoon afterward ran a shop on Dedham Street, South End.

"On Bromfield Street there were the Goodwin Brothers, under the Horticultural Hall.

"Deacon Bates had a shop on Province Street. James Keleher, the grainer, worked for him. On School Street was Thomas D. Morris of blue zinc fame.

"This is a rambling statement, but I shall be pleased if it helps you.

"JAMES HARRISON."

W. & W. J. McPherson.

Among the best practical workmen who ever started in business in Boston were Walter and Wm. J. McPherson, who came to Boston in the early forties. Their names appear in the Boston Directory in 1847. They were then located at 22 School Street, and conducted a general painting and decorating business. They were Scotchmen of unusual ability. Among the miniature painters of Boston, 1847, appears the name of W. J. McPherson.

These brothers were apprentices to Hay of Edinburgh, Scotland, who was probably the most expert painter Scotland ever produced. He could paint pictures, and he was an expert grainer and marbler, and is said to have been the inventor of steel graining combs. Previous to his invention the combs were made of bone or leather. Both McPhersons were skilful grainers and marblers and did much graining for the trade.

Walter McPherson died previous to 1860, and his brother, Wm. J., carried on the business. In 1849, they were located on Derby Range, near Court Street.

About 1862, W. J. McPherson was located at 27 Tremont Row, corner of Pemberton Square, and in 1864 his office was removed to 19 Tremont Street and his shop to 449 Tremont Street. Still later both office and shop were removed to 440 Tremont Street, where they remained until he went out of business about 1900. He died a few years later.

For several years previous to his death, Mr. W. J. McPherson could be consulted by his old customers at the shop of Mr. C. G. Campbell, 10 Clarendon Street, and Mr. Campbell did their work under Mr. McPherson's supervision.

I had a long talk with Mr. McPherson several years before his death, and found him to be evidently both a workman and a gentleman. He always advocated doing work in the best possible manner, and was thus a friend of the journeyman and of the craft. No shop ever established in Boston has done more good for the craft, both master and man, than that of W. J. McPherson. He always advocated the highest grade of work that his clients could afford, and he never rushed his men. He had no legitimate successor.

N. M. Phillips.

In 1850, N. M. Phillips had "Sign Painting Rooms" at 6 Washington Street, near Dock Square. I cannot find that he had any successor. He made a specialty of wooden block letters, "Warranted to last ten times as long without changing their color as those made by machinery."

Chas. A. Codman.

Chas. A. Codman, sign painter, who served his time to J. S. Cloutman, had a shop at 12 Water Street in 1849, and was a well known and excellent workman. The old sign now over the door of Samuel S. Pierce, corner Tremont and Beacon Streets, was painted by him previous to 1855. The work was done for G. Cassell, who had a paint shop at 8 Court Street.

Of the old sign painters of Boston, John Dearborn went to San Francisco where he successfully conducted a sign and carriage painting shop. John Cass went to Chicago, six years ago, and opened a lunch room near the Post Office. Thomas J. Lyford went to Los Angeles, Cal., about 1871, and opened a small sign painting shop. He was alive two years ago.

Conway & Keleher, grainers to the trade, 271 Tremont St., Boston, Mass.

James Keleher learned his trade in Cork, Ireland. He came to Boston in the early fifties, and soon afterward entered the employ of Deacon John Bates. His skill as a grainer was apparent from the first, and he soon began to grain for the trade.

Mr. William Conway was a native of St. John, N.B., and came to Boston in the early sixties. He was an expert grainer, and about 1864 formed a partnership with Mr. Keleher, as Conway & Keleher. Their office was in the shop of John Street, 271 Tremont Street. They were both artists in their line, and their work was in demand all over New England. The partnership was dissolved in the late seventies, each continuing business on his own account.

Mr. Conway died some fifteen years ago, and Mr. Keleher about ten years ago.

Mr. Keleher was one of the most skilful all-round grainers that I have ever met.

William Hopson, grainer.

William Hopson came to Boston in the early fifties, and soon established himself as a grainer to the trade.   He was an excellent workman, and did the graining at the Boston City Hospital in 1858.

He retired from business two years ago, and is now living on a farm in Randolph Centre, Vermont.

William Munroe Ross.

William Munroe Ross came to Boston from Scotland, via New Orleans, about 1854, and was living on West Cedar Street in 1856.   He was an apprentice of Bennett & Bogle of Glasgow, and an expert grainer.   He established himself as a grainer to the trade, removing to River Street, Cambridge, about 1860.   He had an office at 121 Court Street, Boston, for many years.   He died in 1878, aged fifty years.

For several years previous to his death, he studied art, both portrait and landscape painting, making a trip to Europe for this purpose.   Some of his best pictures are in the rooms of the Boston Caledonian Club, of which he was a charter member.

He was succeeded in business by his son, William M. Ross, who also was an expert grainer, and who died March 2, 1905, aged fifty years, leaving no successor.

David A. Granger.

David A. Granger, surveyor of work, was known to many of the old master painters, and did a lucrative business in measuring painted surfaces, where charges were made by the square yard.

In 1849 his office was located at Room 17, Old State House.   One-half the cost of measuring was paid by the painter, and one-half by the owners of the building.   I have seen a bill with this charge added for measuring.

John A. Magee.

John A. Magee started in business at 16½ Leverett Street in the year 1838, and continued in business until 1891, except for a few years when he was sick.   His successors on Leverett Street were Simpson & Barrus, but he started again (after being sick) at 47½ Howard Street.   He died at the age of eighty-three in 1898.

Christopher Needham.

Christopher Needham came to Boston from England in the early sixties, and opened a paint shop.   It is said that he went around to the large (?) houses on the Back Bay, then being rapidly built up, with a bundle of panels and sketches under his arm, and would ring the door bell and ask if the owner wanted any painting or decorating done at the same time exhibiting the samples of his work, which included landscape and marine painting, decorating, graining and marbling. He is said to have secured many desirable customers in this way.

About 1864 he formed a partnership with Lucas Haberstroh, as Haberstroh & Needham. The partnership was dissolved a few years later and Mr. Needham continued business on his own hook.

He retired from business about 1890, and died some ten years ago.

Two notable apprentices from this shop were W. E. Norton, one of America's foremost marine artists, and William F. Halsall, who, after leaving Needham's shop, was a sign painter on Broad Street, and who is now a celebrated marine artist.

Master painters like Christopher Needham are few and far between in these days.

Zachariah Handcock.

Zachariah Handcock is said to have been an apprentice of Thomas D. Morris; at least, he worked for him for many years, and later was established in business as a fresco painter and decorator on Pleasant Street, Boston.

He was one of the members of the first association of master painters in Boston, formed in the late fifties. He died four years ago, and was an honorary member of the Master Painters' Association at the time of his death.

CAMBRIDGE

The records of Christ Church, Cambridge, Mass., built 1759 to 1761, under date of December 9, 1761, show this entry:

"To James Sherman, his account, Painting, £6-14-10:" also, July 4, 1765, "By Paid, Painting the doors, 12s." This entry appears under date of Oct. 13th, 1768: "Paid Joseph Welch for mending 40 squares glass, per discount, £4-16-0:" also, March 4, 1776, "Joseph Welch, his account, for paint and painting the Tinkett, £3-0-0." (Does any one know what the "Tinkett" was?)

A brief space will be taken to describe the doings of Joseph Welch, as he is one of the first master painters in the State of whom I have any record.

The records of the church show that he hired pew No. 31, but the account is still open on the books, showing that he owed over three pounds to the church when he left town, but this did not prevent him from obtaining one pound on account in October, 1774. The charge for painting the "Tinkett" was credited to his account as pew rent.

From a legal friend who has given much time both here and in England to ascertain the history of the early parishioners of Christ Church, I learn the following facts about Joseph Welch.

In 1776 he was suspected of being a loyalist, and was under surveillance;

in 1779, the Committee of Public Safety of New Hampshire wrote a letter to the Committee of Safety of Cambridge, asking that the doings of Mr. Joseph Welch be scrutinized, as he was suspected of being in league with one Baxter of New Hampshire, in the issuance of counterfeit money.

An account filed in London, England, of the claims of the loyalists of New England for compensation for losses sustained by the war, contains the affidavit of Joseph Welch, painter and glazier, of Cambridge, Mass. His claim was for loss of time for each day of the war, next for loss of his house and shop confiscated by the colonists, also for being kept in jail one winter. His claim recites the fact that by his assistance four of Sir John Burgoyne's officers, prisoners of war in Cambridge, were enabled to escape.

His claims were disallowed but he was allowed a small pension, and was provided with a position under the Crown at Shelburne, N.S.

It is on record that before leaving Cambridge, he mortgaged his house to one Porter, and left his family in possession. The deeds describe the house and shop as being close to where the city building in Brattle Square now stands.

J. N. Deer, 17 Fairmont Avenue.

Mr. Deer began business in Cambridge in 1873, with J. Frank Row as a partner, as Row & Deer. Within a year he withdrew from the firm and formed a partnership with Thomas Wilson as Wilson & Deer. This partnership continued for about ten years, when it was dissolved, and each member of the firm opened a shop on his own account. Mr. Deer is still actively in business.

Frank Wilson, 21 Fairmont Avenue.

Mr. Thomas Wilson, the father of the present proprietor, started in business in Cambridge in 1874, with J. N. Deer, as Wilson & Deer. Ten years later the partnership was dissolved, and Mr. Wilson soon after admitted his son Frank into partnership, as T. Wilson & Son.

Mr. Thomas Wilson withdrew from the firm some ten years ago, since which time the firm name has been Frank Wilson. Thomas Wilson died December 22, 1909.

M. A. Feeley, 265 Western Ave.

Mr. Feeley began business in Cambridge on his own account in 1874, and has continued the business without change in the firm, and with but few changes in location since that time. He has made a specialty of decorative work on ceilings and walls of large buildings. He is a past President of the Cambridge Master Painters' Association and served the State Society as President in 1906 and 1907.

John Fulton, Winthrop St.

Mr. Fulton was established in Cambridge about 1820. One of his apprentices was George O. Danforth, who established a shop of his own in 1844. Mr. Danforth died about twenty years ago. His shop has no direct connection with any existing shop.

It is worthy of note that Mr. John Fulton survived his own son, who died over sixty years of age, and Mr. Danforth, his apprentice. He was over ninety years of age at his death.

J. L. & W. B. Holt, Cambridge.

This firm was formed about 1871. Mr. J. L. Holt died about 1873, and W. B. Holt was his successor. At his death, Mr. Thomas Donlan took the shop, and at his death, Mr. J. Fallon, who soon gave up the business. There is no successor. Mr. J. Leo McDonald has the old shop.

H. L. Stewart, Cambridge.

H. L. Stewart was probably an apprentice of Deacon Bates. In 1846 he had a shop at 76 Pleasant Street, Boston, and in 1849 the firm was H. L. Stewart & Co., 62½ Cornhill, Boston.

We next hear of Mr. Stewart in Harvard Square, Cambridge, where he conducted a shop for many years. He died about 1880.

Mr. W. J. Edwards was apprenticed to Mr. Stewart about 1871, and soon after the death of his old master he hired the shop in which he served his time.

CHELSEA

W. E. Lancey.

J. A. Lancey first started a paint shop at 11 and 13 Congress Avenue, Chelsea, in 1870, and it continued to be a paint shop until the big fire April 12, 1908, making it a period of thirty-eight years. The firm was J. A. Lancey, 1870 to 1878, then J. A. Lancey & Son, 1878 to 1885, then Lancey & Brewer, 1885 to 1890, and W. E. Lancey, 1890 to 1908, since which time the business has been discontinued.

STONEHAM

Joseph Stevens and a man named Horton had paint shops in Stoneham in 1855. Mr. Stevens removed to Cambridge about 1860, and was in business there for nearly forty years. He died in Somerville about 1907, aged ninety-two years.

Joe Barrett.

The first painter to open a shop in Stoneham was Joe Barrett. He was a versatile genius and an all around artist. He painted and frescoed churches, painted panoramas and portraits. In the early fifties he ceased to do house painting and applied his talents wholly to portrait painting and photography. He had no successor as his death, which occurred before 1870.

HOLYOKE

Mr. R. G. Neall, 936 Dwight St., Holyoke, Mass., writes me as follows:

"In 1869, a man by the name of Barnes kept a paint shop on High Street, where the Marble Block now stands; in that same year George Avery, a fine painter and grainer, kept a shop on Maple Street. He still lives, and has retired from business, but Mr. Barnes is dead.

"In 1871, Hiram Farnum kept a paint shop on Dwight Street; he retired quite a few years before he died. After he retired John B. Randall kept Farnum's shop; both are now dead. Smith Bugby ran the same shop until the building was torn down and a block built there. Along about 1878 and 1879, two men, Dean and Wheelock, formed a partnership. This was one of Holyoke's largest shops, and held that position for years. They opened their store on Main Street. Later they separated, Dean going to High Street, and Wheelock remaining on Main Street. He died, and his widow and son still run the shop, Mr. Dean, running an art store and paint shop at 320 High Street, where he is today."

MILTON

William Chapman.

Rufus Chapman established a paint shop in Milton about 1866, and conducted it until his death several years ago; he was for many years Chief Engineer of the Milton Fire Department.

His son William is his successor and still carries on the business.

WESTFORD

Joe Wall, Graniteville, Westford, Mass., writes me as follows:

"The first painter in the town that I can find any record of is a man named Abel Prescott. He lived in Westford Centre, and did the painting in this vicinity about one hundred years ago. He died over fifty years ago. The next was George Prescott and a man named George B. Hildreth, commonly called 'Painter Hildreth.' He always was a painter, and carried on the painting business in Westford for over fifty years; I think nearer to sixty years. His son worked with him. I don't think they ever hired more than one or two men. They worked together until the son died, about thirty years ago. Then the old man used to hire some one to help him. They did no wagon or sleigh work; just painted buildings. When the old man started they got their lead dry and ground it in the oil; they also ground the colors and boiled the oil. George B. Hildreth was born in Westford a little over one hundred years ago. He died about twenty years ago in the same town where he was born. He was a painter all his life; he used to work ten, twelve or fourteen hours per day, and in his early days got all the way from one dollar to one twenty-five per day.

"About 1850 there was a painter named Jonas Butterfield, who lived at West Chelmsford, Mass. He ran the painting business for about thirty years, and used to paint in the neighboring towns. My brother and myself bought the stock and tools from the heirs after the old man died. There was a painter, named William Brown, who lived at West Chelmsford, and was in company with Jonas Butterfield at one time. He was a native of England, and was the best all-around painter that ever was in this neighborhood. He learned his trade in the old country. He worked in this village in the machine shop, but wherever he worked he had the name of being first-class in all branches of the painting trade. One man of Westford, who worked with William Brown, was Lester Hamblet. He was a native of this town. I think he began to work with William Brown, and later went to Fitchburg, Mass., and did a big painting business until his death, when the shop was sold to the Fitchburg Hardware Co.

"There is an old painter who lives on the outskirts of the town. He is about seventy years old. He has been painting over fifty years, but he has a farm and does not depend on painting alone. His name is William Dane, and he is a native of Chelmsford, Mass.

"Two other painters who lived here over twenty years ago were William Jolly and Thomas Wing. They were natives of Manchester, England. Both men have been dead for a number of years. Wing died at Newton, and Jolly at Lynn, Mass."

PAINT SHOPS NOW IN OPERATION

NORTH ATTLEBORO

H. B. Cornell, 22 Washington Street, South.

The shop of H. B. Cornell was founded in 1872 by an uncle of the present proprietor, Daniel B. Cornell. In 1876 he took into partnership a brother, Benjamin M. Cornell, after which the concern was known as Cornell Brothers.

In 1879, Henry P. Cornell, the father of the present proprietor, was taken into the firm, and in 1880 a branch store was established in Attleboro.

In 1882, Daniel B. Cornell died, and a few months later the store occupied by them in Guild Block, North Attleboro, was burned out. This entailed a financial loss from which they never recovered, and in 1884 they were compelled to assign for the benefit of their creditors, and the business was practically wound up.

H. B. Cornell, however, continued to do business in a small way until 1892, when his son, the present proprietor, became associated with him. From that time the business has grown steadily, and in 1899, H. B. Cornell, Jr., purchased his father's interest, and has since carried on the business under the name of H. B. Cornell.

Mr. Cornell is a member of the Society of Master House Painters and Decorators of Massachusetts.

BEVERLY

J. V. Porter & Co.

The firm of J. V. Porter & Co. was established in 1853, and the senior member of the firm is still doing business.

H. M. &. R. E. Hodgkins, High Street, Beverly Farms. R. E. Hodgkins writes me as follows:

"The original firm, Hodgkins Bros., of which we are an offshoot, was established about thirty years ago and consisted of Harvey M. Hodgkins and Eli R. Hodgkins. They continued together under the old firm name until 1894. At that time the partnership was dissolved, and the senior member, Harvey M., together with a nephew, Robert E., established the present firm of H. M. & R. E. Hodgkins. In September, 1906, H. M. Hodgkins died. Since then R. E. has, through the various ups and downs of our mutual trade, conducted the business under the same firm name. We fancy our name is as well known (and we hope as favorably) on the North Shore as any engaged in the business. We have tried to associate it with honest dealing and good work."

BOSTON, MASS.

George B. Agnew, 87 Warren Street, Roxbury.

William Agnew was born in Calais, Maine, in 1837; learned his trade in St. Andrews, N.B. Coming to Boston in 1855, he went to work for J. J. Munroe on Warren Street, and in 1858 he started in business at the corner of Eustis and Dearborn Streets, under the name of William Agnew & Co., his partner being a man named John C. Palfrey. The partnership continued about a year and a half, and the location was changed to Champney Place, also to Warren Street, near Washington. He came to 87 Warren Street, its present location, in 1879.

In 1887, Geo. B. Agnew was admitted to partnership, and the firm became William Agnew & Son, and so continued until the death of the senior partner in March, 1903. Mr. Nelson Agnew, brother of George B., was admitted to partnership in the same year, and the firm was continued as Agnew Bros., until April, 1909, Nelson Agnew withdrawing from the firm. George B. Agnew is now carrying on the business at the old stand.

Mr. Agnew is a member of the Boston Master Painters' Association.

The American Painting & Decorating Co., 126 Milk Street.

This firm is the outgrowth of a business established at 91 Chapman Street, by the father of C. G. Campbell, the present president of the company. The shop was established about 1878, and in 1885 Mr. C. G. Campbell succeeded his father, who retired from the business and died about 1903.

The shop was removed to Warren Avenue, and later to 10 Clarendon Street, where it remained for several years. Later Mr. Campbell became manager, and still later president of the American Painting and Decorating Co., first located at 40 Batterymarch, and now at 126 Milk Street, where the firm occupy a whole building.

This firm takes many contracts for large buildings, in various parts of the country, and employs a large staff of mechanics. They are members of the Master Builders' Association and the Master Painters' Association.

George W. Brooks, 165 Warren Street, Roxbury.

Mr. George W. Brooks writes me as follows:

"This shop was established in the year 1849, by J. J. Munroe, who, as near as I can find out, worked for a Mr. Luther Noyes in 1844, who removed to Castle Street in 1850, and was there until 1863. Mr. Munroe retired in 1879, after thirty years in business, and was succeeded by G. W. Downs, who carried on the business until his death in 1892, thirteen years, when I bought out the business, March 31, 1892, and have carried it on since, about seventeen years. I worked journey work for both Mr. Munroe and G. W. Downs, and have been in this location thirty-five years or more (and I'm not on Easy Street, yet).

"My father, Adam Brooks, carried on the painting business in Boston sixty years or more ago. It is impossible for me to get the dates of the time he went into business. His shop was on the corner of Dover and Washington Streets, also under the Hub Theatre. He also had a shop where the Grand Opera House is now. He worked for, and I think learned his trade of J. Green, whose shop was on the corner of Lucas and Washington Streets."

Mr. Brooks is an active member and ex-President of the Master Painters' Association of Boston.

D. E. Bryan, 4 East Springfield Street.

Charles H. Knox, the founder of the shop, was born in Portland, Maine, in 1811. He learned the painters' trade, came to Boston, and was in active business over sixty years. In 1846 he was located at 127 Milk Street, in 1850 at 149 Milk Street, and in 1865 his shop was at 8 Province Court.

Mr. Bryan entered the employ of Mr. Knox in 1858, having served his time with A. G. Lyon, who kept a paint shop at 6 Bridge Street, West End. He was foreman for Mr. Knox for many years, and from 1879 was equal partner with him. The firm has been located at East Springfield Street about thirty years.

He was admitted to the Massachusetts Charitable Mechanic Association in 1856, and died in 1891, aged eighty years.

On his death he was succeeded by D. E. Bryan, the present proprietor.

Alan Burke, 207 Green Street, Jamaica Plain.

Alan Burke came to Boston in 1854, and established himself in business in 1862. He has been located at 207 Green Street, Jamaica Plain, for many years, and still gives the business his personal attention, although close to eighty years of age. He has painted several signs in a creditable manner within the last month.

John Cotton & Son, 142 Harrison Avenue.

The business was established about 1834, by Jacob Thaxter, then located at the corner of Harrison Avenue and Beach Street. In 1847 he moved to the corner of Harrison Avenue and Essex Street, admitting John Cotton, his apprentice, to partnership, under the name of Jacob Thaxter & Co. On the death of Mr. Thaxter, in 1848, John Cotton succeeded to the business. In 1871 he removed to 170 Harrison Avenue, where he remained until his death in 1884, when his son took the business, moving to 142 Harrison Avenue, in 1898, where the firm is now located.

N. G. Finney, 110 Portland Street.

A. M. Leech was in Boston in various places in the South End of Boston from about 1850. He retired from business in 1873, and his successor is Nathaniel G. Finney, the old shop being on Common Street. Later Mr. Finney removed to 47 Blossom Street, and is at present located at 110 Portland Street. He is a member of the Master Painters' Association.

L. Haberstroh & Son, 647 Boylston Street.

Lucas Haberstroh, the founder, studied the art of decorating and painting in Germany, where he was born. He afterwards went to England for three years, where he had the opportunity to work on some of the finest baronial mansions.

In 1848 he came to Boston and established his business. He took as partner, K. Kaiser, a friend, who came to this country with him. The firm name was Haberstroh & Kaiser. They also established a branch in Philadelphia.

About the year 1851 two more partners were taken in, under the name of Haberstroh, Kaiser & Lamor.

This firm dissolved partnership after the Boston Theatre was decorated, in 1854 and 1855, when Kaiser and Lamor went to Philadelphia and carried on that branch of the business. The firm in Boston was then Haberstroh & Müller. (D. Müller was brother-in-law of L. Haberstroh.)

Later N. Meyer became a member of the firm under the name of Haberstroh, Müller & Meyer.

The firm dissolved partnership in a few years. D. Müller established himself in Brooklyn, N.Y., as ecclesiastical figure painter and decorator, and L. Haberstroh carried on business alone until about the year 1865, when he formed a partnership with Christopher Needham, at 608 Washington Street, nearly opposite Hollis Street.

The firm dissolved about the year 1870, when L. Haberstroh continued alone at 12 School Street, then at 28 School Street.

In 1877, his son Albert became partner, under the firm name of L. Haberstroh & Son.

In 1883, Lucas Haberstroh died.

The business was removed to 9 Park Street, where it was continued by Albert Haberstroh, sole proprietor, for over twenty years.

In 1905, Albert Haberstroh purchased the building at 647 Boylston Street, where the business is carried on at the present time (1910). Mr. Haberstroh has associated with him, his two sons, Emil F. and Arthur L.

The firm are members of the Boston Master Painters' Association and the Master Builders' Association of Boston.

Hanson & Mouncey, 57 Roxbury Street, Roxbury.

In 1879, C. F. W. Hanson and James Mouncey formed a co-partnership as painters and decorators, both partners being skilled workmen, in ability far above the average. They located in Roxbury, and have occupied their present quarters at 57 Roxbury Street for thirty years or more. Both have been actively identified with the master painters' association, each member of the firm having been honored by the presidency of the Master Painters' Association of Boston, and also of the State Society of Master Painters, Mr. Hanson at the present time being the president of the latter body. While not large employers of labor, this firm has always had the reputation of doing excellent work.

A. W. Knowlton, 5 Chambers Street.

This shop was established by the grandfather of A. C. Longley, very early in the last century. In 1847 we find A. C. Longley in business at 119 Cambridge Street, and at his death his son, Edwin P. Longley, succeeded to the business and continued it up to July 1909, when he died, and Mr. A. W. Knowlton assumed charge and is at present conducting the business.

Knox & Co., 126 Broad Street.

In 1850, S. Q. and J. M. Currier started a sign painting shop on Hanover Street. They were on Howard Street about 1855. In 1859 they were located at 56 Broad Street, and in 1865 they were at the same location. Later they removed to 359 Atlantic Avenue. They were in the vicinity of Fort Hill Square for many years and retired from business about 1897. Their successors are Knox & Co., 126 Broad Street.

Oscar L. Lorentzen, 165 Tremont Street.

Mr. Joshua Sears established himself as painter and decorator about the year 1880 on Mason Street, where he conducted more or less business. His wife also had a studio in a building in the vicinity of the Studio Building. Several years later he removed to 178 Tremont Street, in the basement, where he had office and shop combined. He remained there until the early part of 1903, when the shop was moved to 130 Harrison Avenue and the office to 165 Tremont Street. Mr. Sears died in November, 1903.

In 1904 the business was purchased by Oscar L. Lorentzen, who started with Mr. Sears as an apprentice in 1889, and carried on business under the name of Joshua Sears & Company, until early in 1909, when the name was changed to Oscar L. Lorentzen, Successor to Joshua Sears & Company.

H. Newton Marshall Co., 166 Devonshire Street.

This firm is an offshoot of two older shops. About 1870 James Hewitson left Hastings' shop on Charles Street and opened a shop at the foot of Revere Street. Later he removed to 36 Charles Street. At his death his son Edward succeeded him, and about 1895 Mr. F. E. Cutler purchased the business, and still later he purchased the business of W. A. Rawson. He took into partnership Mr. H. Newton Marshall and formed a corporation under the name of Cutler-Marshall Co. The shop was at 54 Charles Street. In 1906 Mr. Marshall purchased Mr. Cutler's interest in the corporation and changed the name to H. Newton Marshall Co.; office, 166 Devonshire Street.

Mr. Cutler started a new business on his own account. The firm are members of the Boston Master Painters' Association and the Master Builders' Association of Boston.

Frank W. McCormack, 137 Worcester Street.

James McCormack and Lucius Poole, both of whom worked for Cyrus T. Clark, started in business April 12, 1870, at 596 Washington Street, opposite Hollis Street. January 1, 1871, they removed to 96 Worcester Street, and on January 1, 1877, they removed to 137 Worcester Street, where the shop still stands. January 1, 1888, after the death of Lucius Poole, the firm name was changed to McCormack & Son, and since the death of James McCormack the business has been conducted by Frank W. McCormack. Mr. McCormack is a member of the Boston Master Painters' Association.

John E. Patten, 58 Lenox Street.

John E. Patten, 58 Lenox Street, began business in 1879 at 598 Shawmut Avenue and later removed to 161 West Lenox Street. In 1885 he removed to James Walsh's old shop and from there to 58 Lenox Street, in 1899, where he still continues the business. Mr. Patten also does graining for the trade.

Lewis F. Perry's Sons Co., Paddock Building, 101 Tremont Street.

The business was established by Lewis F. Perry in 1860 at South Dedham, now Norwood. In 1864 Mr. Perry came to Boston, and had a shop and office at 40 Bromfield Street; in 1866 he moved to the corner of Washington and School Streets, and had a shop on the fourth story of the Old Corner Bookstore Building. In 1870 he moved to 43 Temple Place, and in 1875 to Hamilton Place, at the corner of the alley leading through to Winter Street, where he remained until 1886, when he removed to 8 Bosworth Street.

In 1892 he took into partnership his son-in-law, Benjamin Whitney, and the firm name was changed to Lewis F. Perry & Whitney.

In 1898 a corporation was formed, including Lewis F. Perry, Benjamin Whitney and John R. Perry. In 1908 this corporation went out of existence and the present one is the logical successor, Mr. Benjamin Whitney and Mr. E. K. Perry being officers of the corporation, and Mr. John R. Perry, manager.

The firm are members of the Master Builders' Association of Boston.

Peters & Lindsay, 477 Tremont Street.

Secretary Alexander Peters writes me as follows:

"Replying to your letter as to old paint shops, will say that our present location has been in existence as a paint shop since 1869; was first started by James W. Bell, who ran it for six and one-half years, and retired well off to engage in real-estate business. It was continued by his brother, Charles H. Bell, who carried it on with more or less success for about twenty-three years, when he died. The present firm have been at it for the past eleven years.

"This shop was originally an offshoot of William J. McPherson, who was many years located at 440 Tremont Street.

"There was another old firm in this locality, which has since gone the long road, that of Thomas Burgess, who was located at the top of Castle Street."

Mr. Peters is the Secretary of the Master Painters' and Decorators' Association of Boston, Secretary-Treasurer of the Society of Master House Painters and Decorators of Massachusetts, and Chief Organizer of the International Association of Master House Painters and Decorators of the United States and Canada.

Edward Price, 17 Walnut Street, Neponset.

In the year 1873 Mr. Edward Price and Frank L. S. Emery formed a partnership to do painting and decorating under the name of Price & Emery. One year later the firm was dissolved, Mr. Price continuing the business and Mr. Emery starting a shop of his own.

Since 1874 Mr. Price has been located in the same place and is still actively engaged in business, being now the oldest master painter in that locality.

F. M. Rogers & Co., 31 Province Street.

Richard S. Martin had a paint shop at 8 Province Street in 1849 and was probably there many years before that time. Horace Weston was his foreman about 1855. Mr. Martin died about 1861.

Mr. Weston with James R. Putnam formed a partnership under the firm name of Weston & Putnam. This partnership continued for thirty-five years.

Mr. Weston died suddenly in 1896.   Mr. Putnam survived for several years after.

The business was purchased by F. M. Rogers & Co. in March, 1896, and this firm still retains the old shop and are large contractors for painting and decorating.

The firm is composed of F. M. Rogers and his sons, Francis F. and Joseph J.

The senior member of the firm was formerly in the employ of Weston & Putnam.

The firm is a member of the Master Builders' Association.

Horace Weston was born in Plymouth, Mass., in 1825, and learned the painters' trade.   He came to Boston early in life and about 1861 formed a partnership with James R. Putnam, and for over thirty-five years the firm of Weston & Putnam was located on Province Street.   On January 27, 1896, he was stricken while on the street with heart failure and died instantly, aged seventy-one years.   He joined the Massachusetts Charitable Mechanic Association in 1873.

Robert R. Rose, 755 Centre Street, Jamaica Plain.

Mr. Rose established himself in business in Jamaica Plain in 1868, and has continued in business in practically the same location since that date.   He is a member of the Master House Painters' and Decorators' Association of Boston and of the Massachusetts Charitable Mechanic Association.

Shay Bros., 83 Warren Street, Roxbury.

M. F. Shay started alone in the painting business in July, 1872. January 1, 1876, W. E. Shay entered the business. The style of the firm then became and has since continued as Shay Bros. The business was started at 28 Eustis Street, and remained there until March 20, 1880, when the firm bought the painting business of Thomas S. Hodge, who was then, and had been for some twenty years or more, located at 83 Warren Street, Roxbury. Prior to that time Mr. Hodge had conducted the business in the same shop, which was located on the site of the Bank Building, situated on Washington Street, opposite the Dudley Street Station of the Boston Elevated Railway. W. E. Shay had been in the employ of Mr. Hodge for seventeen years, ten of which was in the position of foreman in the same old shop.

Mr. Hodge, when he started in business, had a partner, their firm name being Young & Hodge. J. B. Young afterward retired from painting, and entered the boot and shoe business. After a number of years he went West, and returning to Boston entered the coal and wood business.

For over fifty years Thomas S. Hodge carried on the painting business in Roxbury, and always in the same old shop that is now and has been used by Shay Bros. for over thirty years.

Very few changes have been made in the shop, except putting in a new front and extending the rear to increase floor space, which was done about twenty years ago.

Mr. W. E. Shay died January 6, 1907, and his son, Frederick, was admitted to partnership, the firm name remaining the same.

From the start Shay Bros. have been successful in their business, and they naturally think and pride themselves in the fact that they have the oldest paint shop in Boston.

This firm has been actively identified with the Master Painters' Associations, Mr. M. F. Shay being elected first President of the Society of Master House Painters and Decorators of Massachusetts in 1891, and in 1895 was elected President of the National Association of Master Painters and Decorators. This firm are members of the Massachusetts Charitable Mechanic Association, and carry on a large business.

T. & E. A. Shay, 65 Bartlett Street.

Mr. Thomas Shay established himself in business in Roxbury about 1861, on Dudley Street, near Warren. About 1866 he moved his shop to Bartlett Street, where it is still in operation. Since 1890 his son, Edward, has been a member of the firm. The firm is a member of the Master Painters' Association.

Henry A. Smith, Charlestown.

Henry A. Smith established a paint shop at 278 Main Street, Charlestown, about 1869. He died in 1906, and the shop is now conducted by his brother, under the old firm name.

Thomas F. Sproules, 2 Texas Street, Roxbury.

Thomas F. Sproules opened a paint shop at 2 Texas Street, Roxbury Crossing, in 1877, and has continued in business at the same location since that time.

Mr. Sproules still gives the business his personal attention, and has one of the largest shops in that locality.

Philip Sundell, 1035 Tremont Street.

Philip Sundell and George Dyer formed a partnership in 1876, under the name of Sundell & Dyer, at 162 Cabot Street, Boston. The partnership lasted about eighteen months, Mr. Sundell dissolving the partnership and starting for himself. He has continued the business since that time in his own name, removing to 1057 Tremont Street, and later to 1027 Tremont Street. He does a general painting and decorating business, and in addition conducts a general hardware store, and sells paper hangings. He is a member of the Master Painters' Association of Boston.

Wallburg & Sherry, 136 Harrison Avenue.

In May, 1867, Ottomar Wallburg and William Sherry formed a partnership as painters and decorators. Both were expert workmen as decorators and did much work in this line. Their first shop was at 602 Washington Street, where they stayed for a year. From 1868 to 1869 their shop was at 37 Harvard Street. From 1869 to 1873 they were located at 122 Harrison Avenue. From 1873 to 1886 they were located at 136 Harrison Avenue. From 1886 to 1895 they were located at 114 Harrison Avenue. From 1895 to 1910 they have been located at 136 Harrison Avenue.

Both partners are still actively engaged in the business, and form the oldest copartnership in the painting and decorating trade in Boston.

They have for many years been affiliated with the Master Painters' Association. Mr. Wallburg was President of the Boston Association in 1891. The firm is a member of the Master Builders' Association, also of the Massachusetts Charitable Mechanic Association. Mr. Wallburg is leader of the Master Painters' Orchestra.

William A. Whitney & Son, 132 Broad Street.

The business was established in 1863 at Newburyport, Mass., by William A. Whitney, and continued there for three years, doing house and ship work, and painting some of the finest ships built in those days, for which Newburyport was famous.

In 1866 Mr. Whitney moved the business to South Boston, and continued there for ten years.

In 1876 he moved to Boston, since which time the business has been continued near its present location.

In 1894 Mr. Whitney's son entered into partnership with him, under the firm name of William A. Whitney & Son, and since that time they have been established at their present location, 132 Broad Street. The firm are members of the Boston Master Painters' Association.

George Williams & Son, 3 Province Court.

Balcom & Weston were in business on Pinckney Street previous to 1840. Mr. Weston withdrew from the firm about 1840, and went into business in Groton, Mass.

Mr. George Williams came to Boston in 1841, and entered the employ of Mr. Balcom. He was taken into partnership in 1845, the firm name being Balcom & Williams. The shop was removed to Mt. Vernon Street about 1850, and Mr. Balcom retired from the firm and went into business in Cambridge, Mass., where he was doing business as late as 1869.

Mr. Williams removed his shop to 33 Province Street about 1868, and has been located on Province Street or Province Court for the past forty-two years. The shop is now at 3 Province Court.

In 1907 Mr. Williams took his son, J. D. L. Williams, into partnership.

Mr. Williams, Sr., attends daily to his business, and will be eighty-eight years of age in May, 1910, having been born in 1822. He is undoubtedly the oldest master painter in Boston actively engaged in business, and probably the oldest in the State. He joined the Massachusetts Charitable Mechanic Association in 1891.

James I. Wingate & Son.

In 1854 James I. Wingate came to Boston from Maine, and entered the employ of Chas. S. Burgess, whose shop at that time was on Hawley Street. The Boston Directory for 1847 shows that Chas. S. Burgess then had a shop on Franklin Place.

In 1860 Mr. Burgess admitted into his business his brother, T. H. Burgess, and James I. Wingate, the firm being C. S. Burgess & Company, located in Arch Street. January 1, 1861, the senior partner, Mr. Chas. S. Burgess, retired from the firm and from the business, and the firm became then Burgess & Wingate, and continued as such until 1866, located in Arch Street, and then at corner of Tremont and Castle Streets.

In 1866 the firm was dissolved, and James I. Wingate located at 136 Harrison Avenue, continuing there until 1895. Mr. Wingate's son, F. E. Wingate, was admitted to partnership in 1893; since which date the firm has been James I. Wingate & Son, first at 338 Boylston Street, and now (1910) at 402 Boylston Street, where they have an entire building, and supply furniture, hangings, carpets and decorations for public buildings and private residences, as well as executing all kinds of painting and decorating. The senior partner is still hale and hearty, and personally directs the multifarious operations of his firm.

Mr. T. H. Burgess conducted business for several years after the dissolution of partnership, and was later succeeded by Walter McCreary, who retired from business about 1902, and died a year ago. McCreary's old shop, 9 Lime Street, is now conducted by G. J. Farley. The firm are members of the Master Painters' Association of Boston and of the Boston Master Builders' Association, also Massachusetts Charitable Mechanic Association.

Worthylake & Eagles, 60 Charles Street.

This shop was established by Frank Wallburg and Henry Woehrn in 1879, and they continued in partnership until 1909, when Mr. Woehrn retired.

Ill health caused Mr. Wallburg to dispose of his business; and he sold out to Worthylake & Eagles, the latter having acted as foreman in the shop, and the former already had an established painting and decorating business in Davis Square, West Somerville.

Mr. Wallburg is an ex-President of the Master Painters' Association of Boston.

SIGN PAINTERS.

Warren J. Appleton Sign Co., 49 Cornhill.

Warren J. Appleton began business as a sign painter in 1856, his first shop being at 22 Franklin Street. From 1860 to 1868 he was located first at 4 Washington Street and later at 30 Washington Street. From 1869 to 1878 his shop was at 75 Devonshire Street. A portion of this time Mr. Edgar J. Aveling was his partner.

From 1879 to 1900 the shop was at 292 Washington Street. From 1900 to 1905 the firm was located on Tremont Row, and from 1905 to 1910 at 49 Cornhill. Mr. Appleton still gives his work his personal supervision.

About 1860 Mr. Appleton had the contract to paint the iron fence surrounding Boston Common.

J. L. Blackmer & Co., 380 Atlantic Avenue.

In September, 1866, Mr. J. L. Blackmer opened a shop for sign painting at 4 Merrimac Street. In 1867 Mr. A. A. Lawrence was taken into the firm as partner. The partnership continued until 1874. Mr. Lawrence retired and opened a shop of his own.

Mr. Blackmer removed in 1890 to 96 Court Street, and about 1900 he located at 380 Atlantic Avenue, where he is still actively engaged in business.

He is a life member of the Massachusetts Charitable Mechanic Association, and a past President of the Sign Makers' Association of Boston.

Charles Cabot, 46 North Street..

"Henry Cabot, Sign and Fancy Painter, at the Sign of the Golden Ball," established a paint shop in Scollay's Building in March, 1833. Two years later, in 1835, he went to Blackstone Street, which had recently been reclaimed as a part of the Middlesex Canal, which ran from Boston to Lowell. In 1847 the Directory states that he had a shop on Blackstone Street, near Hanover. He remained here until about 1860. Mr. Charles Cabot, the son of Henry, entered his father's employ January 1,1862, and on the death of his father succeeded to the business, the shop being moved in 1862 to 46 North Street, where it still remains. The firm has always made a specialty of signs, but of late years has done general painting in addition to signs.

"The Golden Ball," Loring's Tavern, was in Merchants Row, corner of Corn Court, in 1777. It was kept by Mrs. Loring in 1789.

Hewes & Mayo, 31 Cornhill.

Lyford & Boyce had a paint shop at 10 Broad Street in 1864, and did much sign work. Later they removed to 61 Cornhill, where for many years they did lettering of all sorts, also house painting.

Mr. Lyford withdrew from the firm about 1878, and A. P. Boyce continued the business. About 1881 he sold out to A. A. Lawrence, who died a few years later. Mr. Boyce was the author of "The Art of Lettering," a standard work.

James B. Hewes, an apprentice of A. P. Boyce, formed a partnership with Harry Hunting, as Hunting & Hewes, and located in the old shop of A. P. Boyce. Later the firm of Hewes & Mayo was formed, who still continue in the old shop. Mr. Hewes retired from the firm and Mr. Mayo withdrew, but the firm name remains.

Mr. E. W. Boyce writes as follows:

"MADISON AVENUE HOTEL, NEW YORK CITY, December 29, 1909.

"*Dear Sir:* Your favor received some time ago, and I trust you will pardon the delay in answering it. I have been away for some time.

"My father, A. P. Boyce, is living with me here in New York winters, and at Cushing's Island, Maine, in the summer. He is eighty years old, enjoys very good bodily health, but his mind is somewhat poor and his memory bad. As far as I can remember I will tell you about his business.

"I have often heard him speak of being in business with a man named Holmes, in the old Gerrish Market (on Sudbury Street, I think he said), and of being burned out there. After that he and Mr. Thomas J. Lyford opened a place on Broad Street under the name of Lyford & Boyce, and did a good business there until the big Boston fire burned them out in 1872. About a year or so before this time Lyford withdrew, and later went West, to Los Angeles, Cal., where I believe he now is. Several years ago, while traveling in Southern California, one winter, my father stopped at Los Angeles and called on him. He was keeping a small shop, and doing enough business to keep himself busy. My father used to write him occasionally up to about a year ago, but has not done so since then.

"After the big fire he opened a place at 65 Cornhill, under his own name, A. P. Boyce. His business grew rapidly, and in about a year or two he hired the building at 31 Cornhill, letting the store and basement, and using the rest. Here he remained for many years, doing a large business in both sign and house painting. He had several apprentices during this time who turned out well, and afterward opened small places of their own and have done well. He did a lot of swing stage work, and most of the other painters would send their work of this kind to him.

"About 1886 or 1887 my brother and I went into the hotel business, having a house in Florida and the Massapoag Lake Hotel at Sharon, Mass., and we induced our father to retire and live with us.

"At that time Mr. Harry A. Hunting was his foreman, and James B. Hewes assistant, and together they bought the business and ran it under the name of Hunting & Hewes. After a few years Hunting died and Hewes then took in with him a Mr. Mayo, and the name was changed to the Hewes-Mayo Sign Co. After a time Hewes left the concern and went to

England, opening a sign painting shop in London, but returned later on, and is now running a shop on Cornhill, as the American Sign Co. Mayo left the concern before Hewes did, and went into another business in the West, I think.

"The old place at 31 is still running, but the business is very small compared with what it used to be, and I do not know who is running it, but think it is still called the Hewes-Mayo Co.

"When my father was in business there were only a few good shops in Boston, but there are lots of them now, and many poor ones, I am told.

"Beside the sign business my father published several art books and derived quite a revenue from them. The best known ones among sign painters were 'The Art of Lettering and Sign Painters' Manual' and the 'Modern Ornamenter and Interior Decorator,' 'Boyce's Manual of Ornament and Banner Painter.' Among fresco painters, 'Boyce's Fresco and Decorative Designs,' and two 'Collection of Ornaments,' Books 1 and 2.

"After giving up business he traveled a good deal, both in this country and abroad, and whenever he could get the chance he would inspect the various sign shops. He was especially interested in those he saw in London, Paris, Berlin and Havana.

"When I asked him if he remembered Mr. Wall, he said he did but could not place him. I am sorry I cannot give you more information concerning his shops. He would be very glad to do so himself if he could remember, but I am sorry to say he cannot.

"During his life he painted many pictures, landscapes, marines, fruits, etc., several of them being placed on exhibition in art galleries at different times. He only did this for the pleasure it gave him, and his love for such work, and would never sell any of them. I have most of them in my own home now.

"If you are in New York at any time I would be pleased to have you call on me. If I can help you further, let me know.

"Hoping that some of what I have written may be of use to you, I remain,

"Yours very truly,

"E. W. Boyce."

GRAINERS

Fred Cathcart, 16½ Union Square, Somerville, Mass.

Edmund Wall began business as a grainer to the trade in 1869, on Oak Street, Somerville. A year later he removed to 22 Murdock Street, Cambridgeport. In 1871 Henry C. Walker of Birmingham, England, was admitted to partnership, the firm being Wall & Walker. Mr. Walker retired early in 1872, and Edmund Wall died December 12, 1874, leaving the business to his son.

William E. Wall, grainer and sign painter, lived from October, 1875, to September, 1885, at 12 Brewer Street, Cambridge. In September,

1885, he removed to the corner of Cambridge and Prospect Streets, Cambridgeport, and in July, 1886, he removed to 14 Morgan Street, Somerville. The sign painting was omitted. In 1903 he opened an office at $16\frac{1}{2}$ Union Square, Somerville.

On April 1, 1909, Mr. Wall retired from the graining business to enter the employ of the N. Z. Graves Co. of Philadelphia, as New England representative for the Brankin brand of colors, varnishes and white lead.

Mr. Fred Cathcart, who for eleven years was Mr. Wall's assistant, purchased the business April 1, 1909, and has continued it since that time. He is Secretary-Treasurer of the Grainers' Association of Boston and Vicinity.

Francis A. Hartford, 57 Gates Street, South Boston.

Mr. Hartford has done graining and sign writing for the trade for the past thirty-five years. He is a member of the Grainers' Association of Boston and Vicinity.

C. A. Morgan, 489 Essex Street, Lawrence, Mass.

Mr. Morgan has been a grainer to the trade since 1878. He is a member of the Grainers' Association of Boston and Vicinity.

John E. Patten, 58 Lenox Street, Boston.

Mr. Patten, in addition to his painting business, does graining for the trade. Mr. Patten is a member of the Grainers' Association of Boston and Vicinity.

W. L. Ricker, 14 Kilby Street, Worcester, Mass.

Mr. Ricker has been a grainer to the trade for the past forty years. He is also a specialist in preparing and coating school blackboards.

Francis Vincent, 12 Fairmount Street, Malden, Mass.

Mr. Francis Vincent has been a grainer to the trade since 1870. He resides at 12 Fairmount Street, Malden, and is President of the Grainers' Association of Boston and Vicinity.

EAST BOSTON

John Brant, 19 Lewis Street.

This shop was established by George Butts previous to 1840. In 1849 Geo. Butts & Son had a shop on Marginal Street, East Boston, and in 1865 their shop was on Marginal Street, near Orleans.

They were succeeded in business by Ithamar Mareen, who moved the shop to 19 Lewis Street, East Boston. Mr. Mareen entered the police 'department as harbor master, and about 1880 C. J. F. Madigan succeeded him in business.

He was in turn succeeded by Mr. John Brant, who began business on his own account in 1878 at 20 Atlantic Avenue, Boston, but later moved his shop to 19 Lewis Street, East Boston, where he still continues in business.

Arthur W. Campbell, 165 Border Street.

John D. Campbell opened a paint shop in East Boston about 1865. For many years the shop was located on Meridian Street, near Lexington Street. Later the shop was moved to 31 Eutaw Street. Mr. Campbell retired from business several years ago, and his son, Arthur W. Campbell, succeeded him and soon afterwards removed the shop to 165 Border Street.

T. H. G. Demott, 7 Gove Street.

H. Busell started in business in the year 1850 in a building then standing about three hundred feet from the present situation of the shop now occupied by his successors. In 1872 he took as partner, H. Hobbs, the partnership lasting about one year, when Mr. Hobbs retired.

Mr. Busell continued the business until his retirement from active participation in 1904, because of old age, after a business career of fifty-four years as painter. He was the foe of adulteration in all things and his greatest boast was that he never failed to pay one hundred cents on the dollar.

The business is now conducted by T. H. G. Demott, who for over thirty years was in Mr. Busell's employ.

N. T. Gorham & Son, 116 Border Street.

Mr. N. T. Gorham, at the age of twenty-two, started in June, 1845, to learn the painting business with the firm of Albertson & Nickerson, at 61 Sumner Street, East Boston, at fifteen dollars a month.

In 1846 there was some misunderstanding and the firm of Albertson & Nickerson dissolved, and N. T. Gorham went with Amasa Nickerson as foreman in his new shop at 29 Sumner Street. After three years, in 1849, Mr. Nickerson was taken sick, and had to give up business, Mr. N. T. Gorham buying him out, and continuing the business under the name of N. T. Gorham. In less than a year, Mr. Nickerson returned and entered the firm, making it Gorham & Nickerson.

January 1, 1866, Amasa Nickerson was again taken sick and N. T. Gorham bought him out again, taking a brother, B. F. Gorham, into the firm, under the name of Gorham Brothers. In 1868 B. F. Gorham's health gave out and Amasa Nickerson bought him out, and entered the firm again, as Gorham & Nickerson. In 1869 N. T. Gorham sold out his interest to Amasa Nickerson, who carried on the business under his own name. In less than a year, N. T. Gorham and B. F. Gorham were back in the shop working and in January, 1871, N. T. Gorham bought out Amasa Nickerson and took his brother, B. F. Gorham, again as partner, making the firm once more Gorham Brothers. In 1875 N. T. Gorham again bought out B. F. Gorham, making the firm N. T. Gorham, and in 1877 N. T. Gorham again sold out to Amasa Nickerson, making the firm again Amasa Nickerson.

In 1878 Amasa Nickerson died, and as N. T. Gorham had to go in the shop and settle up the estate, he bought the shop at the appraiser's price, taking his brother with him, changing the firm again to Gorham Brothers. They continued in business together until 1886, when N. T. Gorham took the business and carried it alone until 1890, when his son, N. T. Gorham, Jr., entered the firm. The firm then became N. T. Gorham & Son. N. T. Gorham, Sr., died February 22, 1907, and his son succeeded to the business under the same firm name.

The firm was located at the old shop that was built for Amasa Nickerson in 1847, until they removed to their new shop at 116 Border Street, in December, 1900.

Mr. N. T. Gorham is a member of the Society of Master House Painters and Decorators of Massachusetts.

Mr. B. F. Gorham conducted business in his own name for many years at a small shop on Border Street. He retired and went to live at his native place on Cape Cod, where he died several years ago.

R. Hodson, Jr., 10–14 Bennington Street.

Mr. Robert Hodson, Jr., writes me as follows:

"In 1846 Robert Hodson started in business in Oxford, Oxfordshire, England. A few years later he transferred his business to Banbury, of the same shire, the home of the famous 'Banbury cakes.' While in Banbury, Mr. Hodson took charge of the entire painting department of the Britannia Works owned by the late Sir Bernard Samuelson.

"In 1872 Mr. Hodson, accompanied by his young son, Robert, sailed for New York. After a tour of the principal cities of the United States and Canada, he settled in East Boston and immediately started in business on Princeton Street. The business increased rapidly, so Mr. Hodson and his five sons (Mr. Hodson's large family had all by this time landed at and were working in East Boston) removed to 30 Bennington Street. About twenty years ago they purchased the commodious property they now occupy at 10–14 Bennington Street, situated in the heart of the business district of East Boston.

"A unique sign and one which attracted attention for years read 'Hodson and Five Sons: Efficient workmen sent to all parts of the world.'

"Mr. Hodson had a family of eight girls and five boys. The boys were all brought up in the business, and like their father were, and are now, one and all, practical all-round workmen.

"Mr. R. Hodson, Sr., who is nearing the four score and ten mark, is well and hearty, and is thoroughly enjoying life. He likes nothing better than to roll up his sleeves to take charge of the business when his son, Robert, has to be away from the shop."

Mr. Hodson is a member of the Master Painters' Association.

SOUTH BOSTON

R. B. Beven & Co., 263 Fourth Street.

The business was established at 4 Lowell Place, now Tamworth Street, March 22, 1877. On February 1, 1879, it was moved to 37 Harrison Avenue, corner of Beach Street, and in 1885 to 263 Fourth Street, South Boston, the present location. Mr. Beven is a past President of the South Boston Master Painters' Association.

H. O. Goodwin, 459 Broadway.

Mr. H. O. Goodwin established a paint shop in 1879 at the corner of F and Third Streets.

A few months later he removed his shop to 459 Broadway, where it still remains. Mr. H. A. Goodwin is now associated with his father in the business. The firm is a member of the Master Painters' Association of South Boston.

N. T. Howard & Son, 148 F Street.

The business was established May 1, 1871, under the firm name of Howard & LeCain. This partnership lasted only one year, then changed to Whitney & Howard, and continued until 1876, when the firm dissolved and shortly afterward became Howard & Worthylake. Upon the death of Mr. Worthylake the business was continued under the name of N. T. Howard, and so continued until the present partnership, which was established in 1896, when his son, Mr. Frank E. Howard, was admitted into partnership.

With the exception of two years under Whitney & Howard, when the shop was on Foster's Wharf, the business has been carried on in the same block on F Street.

The firm are members of the South Boston Master Painters' Association, Mr. Frank E. Howard being a past President of the Association, and in January, 1909, he was elected Vice-President of the Society of Master House Painters and Decorators of Massachusetts, which office he still holds.

Walter Pritchett, 354 Dorchester Street.

Mr. James Pritchett, a native of Birmingham, England, came to Boston in 1859, and for years worked as a shop grainer. He established himself in the painting business in South Boston in 1872, at 13 Boston Street, taking his son Arthur into partnership, the firm being James Pritchett & Son. Arthur Pritchett died in 1880, and another son, Walter, was admitted to partnership. The shop was removed about 1878 to 43 Ward Street. James Pritchett died in 1902, and the business is now conducted by his son Walter, at 354 Dorchester Street, where it has been located for the past twenty-two years. The firm are members of the South Boston Master Painters' Association.

Francis White, 117 Dorchester Street.

In 1877 Francis White established himself as a painter and decorator at 437 Third Street, South Boston. In 1879 he removed to 117 Dorchester Street, and is still doing business at that location, his shop being one of the best known in South Boston. He is a member of the South Boston Master Painters' Association.

BRAINTREE

Conrad Mischler.

Conrad Mischler, Braintree, Mass., began business in Boston in 1874, corner Dover Street and Harrison Avenue. He removed to Braintree in August, 1876, where he has been located ever since. He is a member of the Society of Master House Painters and Decorators of Massachusetts.

BROCKTON

L. Richmond & Co., 65 Main Street.

Lucius Richmond established a paint shop in Brockton about 1850. At the outbreak of the Civil War he went to the front as Captain of a battery of artillery, taking with him Richard Holland and John H. Lamson, two of his apprentices. They all survived the war. Captain Richmond retired as Major, and resumed his business. He died several years ago, and the business is now conducted by his sons.

BROOKLINE

James H. Boody, 204 Washington Street.

James H. Boody started in business in Brookline in the year 1868. The changes in the firm have been as follows: From 1868 to 1873, J. H. Boody; from 1873 to 1879, Harrison & Boody. (Mr. Harrison is still alive in Stoneham, but is not in business.) From 1879 to 1910, J. H. Boody. In this time the business has been conducted in practically the same location. Mr. Boody is a member of the Massachusetts Charitable Mechanic Association.

Hand Bros., 200 Washington Street.

The business was established in 1856, under the firm name of Hand
& Smith. Their place of business was in what was known as the
Mahoney Building on Washington Street. It has since been torn down.
The firm was dissolved in 1860, and the business carried on under the
name of J. B. Hand, at 32 Boylston Street, where it remained until 1867,
when it was removed to its present quarters, 200 Washington Street.
Since the death of Mr. J. B. Hand, in 1900, the business has been carried
on by his sons under the firm name of Hand Brothers. James B. Hand
was born in St. John's, Newfoundland. He came to Boston when young,
and learned the trade of a house painter in Brookline, where he lived
fifty-seven years. He was for many years a selectman of the town, also
an overseer of the poor, and held other offices of trust. He was a member
of the Boston Master Painters' Association and of the Massachusetts
Charitable Mechanic Association in 1882. He died in 1900, aged
seventy-one.

Daniel Hunt, 42 Washington Street.

The paint shop of which Mr. Daniel Hunt is the successor was estab-
lished in Brookline Village in 1815, by Silas Snow. In 1845 Mr. Snow
admitted to partnership Mr. B. F. Baker, the firm being Snow & Baker.
In 1847 Mr. Farrington was admitted to membership, the firm being
Baker & Farrington. On the retirement of Mr. Farrington, in 1864,
the firm was changed to B. F. Baker. The shop was conducted by
B. F. Baker until 1899, when the firm name was changed to B. F. Baker
& Company. In 1902 a former employee of Mr. Baker, Mr. Daniel
Hunt, succeeded B. F. Baker & Company, and now conducts this
ancient shop at 42 Washington Street. Benjamin F. Baker was born in
Kennebunk, Maine, in 1820. He learned the painters' trade and came
to Brookline in 1843. He was town clerk of Brookline from 1852 almost
till the time of his death. He was a member of the State Legislature,
Trustee of Savings Bank, and held many other offices, especially clerical,
as he was a fine penman. He joined the Massachusetts Charitable
Mechanic Association in 1856, and died in 1898, aged seventy-eight.

CAMBRIDGE

John L. P. Ackers, 515 Massachusetts Avenue, Cambridgeport.

John L. P. Ackers was born in Boston in 1836, and went to Rockland,
Maine, at the age of ten years, where he learned the trade of his uncle,
George L. Phillips. Returning to Boston, he was first employed by
"Old Johnny Green," a well-known painter at that time. After several
years in his employ he went into the employ of Mr. Charles A. Sawyer
of Cambridge, and was foreman of that shop for many years. He enlisted
in the army in 1861 and served faithfully.

About 1871, in partnership with Charles Fillebrown, he established the shop of Ackers & Fillebrown, where his signs on the outside of the building, "Putty up, July, Putty down, January," attracted considerable attention. This partnership was dissolved several years after, and Mr. Ackers went again into the employ of Charles A. Sawyer as foreman. In 1882 he left Mr. Sawyer's employ, and established his present business with office and shop at 515 Massachusetts Avenue.

Mr. Ackers died seven years ago, and his son, Charles H. Ackers, has managed the business since that time. The firm is a member of the Master House Painters' and Decorators' Association of which the senior Mr. Ackers was first Secretary and later President.

W. J. Edwards, 28 and 85 Boylston Street.

Mr. W. J. Edwards writes me as follows:

"Replying to yours in regard to the paper on the 'Oldest Paint Shops in Massachusetts,' which you are writing for the next convention of the Massachusetts Society Master House Painters and Decorators, would say that the shop I shall write of is down and out, but the business of that shop is still continued.

"The shop in which I served my apprenticeship was situated in the rear of 22 Boylston Street, Cambridge. It was a two and a half story building that in its palmy days had evidently been a dwelling. The upper floor was used for glazing and painting blinds. In those days the painter was often a practical glazier, for at that time very few, if any, factory-glazed sashes were in existence. I don't know when it became customary to buy ready-glazed windows, but it must have been some time after I started to learn the trade.

"In painting blinds a great deal of Paris green was used, and any one who knows what that meant may be thankful it has been superseded by other materials. For in addition to the deviltry of the pigment in oil, one was apt to contract a dose of painters' colic.

"In those days the mortar and pestle and the paint mill were especially reserved for the apprentice, but I am thankful they were soon to be consigned to the scrap heap.

"The modern extension ladder and many other labor-saving devices and tools were not known. As to these one might write a book. Some of the older painters could write very interestingly of what the painter had to contend with forty or fifty years ago. I hope they are here today. They are more ancient and better qualified to do so than I am.

"How far back that old shop as a paint shop dated I do not know. To the best of my belief it was run by old John Fulton. And from what I have heard him tell and the reputation he gained, he must have been a grinder and a rusher. He ground and rushed himself, for he has told me that he was in the shop at four in the morning, grinding lead and mixing the paints for his workmen to go to their jobs when they started to work.

"He was succeeded by Mr. Henry L. Stewart, the man I served my apprenticeship under. Mr. Stewart was a genuine Down East Yankee. He was more considerate than his predecessor, and a very good man to work for. I believe that he either served his time or worked for a certain Deacon Bates, a prehistoric painter of Boston.

"During my apprenticeship I took charge of Mr. Stewart's books, and I have two in my possession now. They are very interesting to read, especially if one likes to compare prices of materials and methods of figuring work, for many jobs were completed and bills rendered as per measurements. I know of cases where the owner disputed the bill, with the result that a sworn surveyor had to measure the work, the painter and owner each paying one-half the fees. The surveyor often made more square yards than the bill first rendered, but the owner had to settle by the surveyor's measurements.

"I know that Mr. Stewart was in business in the old shop in 1861. I started to learn the trade in 1871, and went in business for myself either in 1875 or 1876. The reason for my doing so, so soon after becoming a journeyman, was that the old boss had promised to take me in partnership, which financial reasons prevented him from doing.

"So far as my 'shop' is concerned, I have moved four times, and after occupying the old building for some years, it was torn down to make way for improvements.

"There is not much that I need say personally. I have had a good many apprentices, some of whom are in successful business today. While the subject of 'Old Paint Shops' is interesting, it is with the living master painters that we must deal, and to those who make the trade better I wish success. What Master Painters' Associations stand for is the line to follow to that end.

"Sincerely yours,
"W. J. Edwards."

William F. Gilbert Painting & Decorating Co., 72 Inman Street, Cambridgeport.

In 1866, Wm. F. Gilbert, who had recently left the employ of J. H. & J. P. Thayer, formed a partnership with John Clarkson of Somerville, under the name of Clarkson & Gilbert. This partnership was dissolved in 1867, both members of the firm then being in Somerville. Mr. Clarkson withdrew from the firm, and the business was continued by Wm. F. Gilbert.

In 1870 he opened a shop on Inman Street, Cambridgeport, and has continued in that locality for the past forty years.

About 1893 he opened a shop on Richmond Street, Boston, which he managed in conjunction with his Cambridge shop.

In 1899 his son, Geo. B. Gilbert, was admitted to partnership, and in 1909 the firm was incorporated as the Wm. F. Gilbert Painting & Decorating Co.

Mr. Wm. F. Gilbert was a past President of the Society of Master House Painters and Decorators of Massachusetts, a past President of the Boston Master Painters' Association, and a past President of the Cambridge Master Painters' Association, a member of the G.A.R., and of many fraternal societies. He died December 15, 1909, aged sixty-eight years, and is succeeded in business by his sons, George B. and James H. Gilbert.

George W. Hughes, 375 Green Street.

This shop was established by Geo. H. Hughes, who left the shop of J. H. & J. P. Thayer about 1877.

He died several years ago, and the business is now conducted at the same place, by his son, Geo. W. Hughes.

John C. Sheafe, 295 Franklin Street.

Charles S. Brookings and John C. Sheafe formed a copartnership in 1869 to do painting and decorating. Their first shop was in the building corner Main and Prospect Streets, Cambridgeport. Later they removed to the building on Western Avenue, occupied partly by Kelley & McKinnon, carpenters. The partnership was dissolved in February, 1881, each conducting his own shop. Mr. Brookings has since retired from business, but Mr. Sheafe is still actively engaged, having his shop corner Franklin Street and Western Avenue, Cambridgeport, where he employs from five to fifteen journeymen.

J. H. & J. P. Thayer & Co., 636 Massachusetts Avenue, Cambrigdeport.

Established 1790. Thomas Thayer was born in England in 1600. Having contracted the emigration fever, so prevalent at that time, he came to this country about 1630, in quest of fairer fields and pastures new, and in 1636 was admitted "freeman," and received title of lands. Richard, a descendant of his, came to Cambridge about 1790, and settled on River Street, on the right-hand side, close to where now stands the Riverside Press. There he opened what was probably the first "Interior and Exterior Decorating" concern (as we say now) in these parts. In those days they called it plain "Paint Shop." If the records are correct, a unique feature of the business was the selling of paint to the "noble red man," wherewith to decorate his classic brow; probably one of the first jobs of "fresco" work done in this country, or was it "Exterior Decoration"? A few years later he moved to the Causeway, now leading to West Boston Bridge, about half a mile west of the same, and about opposite the present office of Geo. W. Gale & Co., on Main Street. At that time no bridge was in existence, but a ferry at the site of the present bridge conveyed people across the "winding Charles" to Charles Street, Boston.

In 1821 he fell a victim of painters' colic, and was succeeded by his second son, Richard, who managed the business until 1833, when his career was cut short by a fall from a swing stage on the north side of the Unitarian Church at Old Cambridge. On the stage with him were Mr. Nathan Walton, an old timer in the business, and James H. Thayer, a younger brother of Richard, who immediately assumed charge of the business under his own name, and took a shop at the corner of Brattle Street and Palmer Court.

Later on, circumstances calling him to other parts of the country, he sold out and opened a shop at Charleston, S.C., where he remained a year, then, returning to Cambridge, he hired quarters where Union Hall formerly stood, on Massachusetts Avenue. After this he conducted a shop at 744 Broadway, New York, where he remained one year, then back to Cambridge, and erected a shop building on Brighton Street (now Boylston) opposite where Hyde's planing mill stood. This being destroyed by fire, he went back to the old location at Brattle Street and Palmer Court.

Late in 1841 we find him in the old Douglass Block, corner Essex and Main Streets (now Massachusetts Avenue), and in 1844, taking in his younger brother, Joshua P., they created the firm of J. H. & J. P. Thayer, and built another shop at 712–714 Massachusetts Avenue, formerly Main Street.

J. P. Thayer, the junior member of the firm of J. H. & J. P. Thayer, was of an adventurous, roving disposition, at one time going on a three years' whaling voyage to the Pacific, and in 1849, leaving Boston on the ship *Sweden*, he sailed around Cape Horn, and was then driven back into the Atlantic. A second attempt was more successful, and finally, after a five months' passage, he reached San Francisco. In all that passage they were spoken but once. Shortly after his arrival, his partner sent out a consignment of glazed sash, which were sold immediately and at extravagant prices. The exposure and severity of working in the mines did not agree with him, and he found employment at his trade of house painting, receiving such high prices as would make the painter of today stare in amazement. After two and a half years' stay, he concluded Cambridge was good enough for him, and so returned via the Isthmus, where he contracted malaria, which did not leave him for many a year.

In 1867 the firm built a four-story building on the westerly side of the lot on Massachusetts Avenue, and moved the shop to this building, where it remained until 1909, when the building was remodeled into a dwelling house, the shop being removed to 842 Main Street, with office at 636 Massachusetts Avenue.

Joshua P. Thayer died about 1876 and James H. Thayer about 1881. Mr. Farwell J. Thayer, son of James H., was admitted to the firm in 1872, and succeeded his father and uncle, retaining the old firm name. In 1901 Mr. Farwell E. Thayer, son of Farwell J., was admitted to partnership, and the firm is at present composed of these two members.

The firm have been actively identified with the Master Painters' National and State Societies, Mr. F. J. Thayer being one of the delegates to the first National Convention at Chicago, in 1885. He is a past President of the Cambridge Master Painters' Association, and was the second Treasurer of the State Society, and continued in office until, at his recommendation, the offices of Secretary and Treasurer were combined.

I append a partial list of journeymen painters who have left Thayer's shop to go into business for themselves:

About 1845, N. Walton; 1855, Jesse Sawyer (later C. A. Sawyer); 1856, Geo. W. Stacy; 1866, Wm. F. Gilbert; 1870, James H. Heffernan; 1871, David Heffernan; 1873, Row & McCoy (later Row & Deer, and James N. Deer); 1873, Rolfe Bros., North Cambridge; 1874, Thos. Wilson (later Wilson & Deer and Frank Wilson); 1874, M. A. Feeley; 1875, J. D. Ford; 1875, Dr. Morley; 1876, John Hicks; 1877, Geo. H. Hughes; 1877, John Mahoney; 1878, Martin Fallon; 1879, John Fallon; 1880, Geo. Dillman; 1880, Ruel W. Hussey; 1884, Geo. Dunn; 1886, E. Gunion de Belle Isle; 1890, Bushee & Compton; 1890, C. C. Lougee; 1892, F. E. Woods; 1895, Chas. H. Cox; 1896, Wilson & Johnson.

This is by no means a complete list, but shows how many firms have been offshoots of this ancient shop.

J. H. Thayer was an alderman of Cambridge in 1861 and 1863, and also held other public offices.

DUXBURY

Previous to 1830 a master painter named Barten carried on business in Duxbury, Mass. About 1830 there were three master painters in that town, viz., Alfred Sampson, J. W. Hathaway and Alden Chandler.

Frank M. Davis, Duxbury.

In 1870 Mr. E. E. Chandler and his brother, J. B. Chandler, started in business in Duxbury, under the firm name of J. B. & E. E. Chandler. J. B. Chandler died in 1885, and from that time E. E. Chandler carried on the business until 1907, when he sold out to Frank M. Daws of Island Creek in Duxbury, who still continues the business.

FALL RIVER

George E. Hoar & Son, 68 Bedford Street.

In 1854 Brightman, Unsworth & Luther started in business on Second Street, in the rear of City Hall. In 1858 they were located on Central Street, west of Main Street, and about that time they sold out their business to George E. Hoar, who continued at the same location for about four years, moving from there to 9 Bedford Street. Six years later he moved to 19 Bedford Street, remaining there about five years. He then moved to the alley near the police station, now Granite Street, staying there about three years, when he moved to his present location, then 45 Bedford Street, now 68, in the fall of 1882. January 1, 1890, George W. Hoar was admitted to partnership, and the name changed to George E. Hoar & Son. December 10, 1899, George E. Hoar died and the business has since been carried on by George W. Hoar under the old name of George. E. Hoar & Son. The firm is a member of the Master Painters' Association.

P. P. Morris, 385 Spring Street.

Mr. Morris began business about 1876 and for a time was partner with Mark A. Sullivan. Since 1880 Mr. Morris has conducted the business in his own name. He is a member of the Master Painters' Association.

Mark A. Sullivan Co., rear 23 Rodman Street.

Mark A. Sullivan started in business in the year 1870 with a man named Peckham, under the firm name of Peckham & Sullivan. About a year after he bought Peckham out, and continued in the business alone. In those two years his shop was on Ninth Street. In 1876 he formed a partnership with P. P. Morris, under the name of Sullivan & Morris. In 1880 the firm dissolved and went into separate shops. Mr. Sullivan then opened a store on Spring Street, with a partner named Harrington, under the firm name of Sullivan & Harrington. Mr. Harrington left the firm in 1882, and Mr. Sullivan moved his shop to 275 South Main Street, where he continued in the painting business until 1890. He then started a side line of furniture. He sold out the furniture business in 1908, and is still continuing the painting business at rear of 23 Rodman Street. Mr. Sullivan is a member of the Fall River Master Painters' Association.

FITCHBURG

George Buckley, 11 and 13 Cushing Street.

The business was established originally by Oliver and Edward Blood in the spring of 1856. They sold out to J. D. Bickford & Co. (J. D. Bickford and Stephen H. Bickford) in 1868, and they carried on business until March 31, 1885, when they sold out to George Buckley & Co. (George Buckley and Joseph Welch), who carried on the business until April 1, 1887, when George Buckley bought out his partner's interest and ran the business until June 1, 1908, when he closed out his business to take a little needed rest.

Since taking the business up alone, Mr. Buckley made three changes in location. His first location was a room or shop over Michael Hogan's blacksmith shop. In 1889 the shop had to be moved to widen the street, and he moved his business to a room over J. Cushing & Company's storehouse, moving only about fifty feet from his old stand, and having a great deal better and larger shop. In 1899 he moved again, just across the street, about seventy-five feet, to 11 and 13 Cushing Street, where he remained until June 1, 1908, when he closed out for a rest.

Mr. Buckley is a member of the Fitchburg Master Painters' Association.

FRAMINGHAM

A. G. Priestly, Saxonville.

The business was established by Thomas A. Priestly, who came from Leeds, England, to Boston in August, 1848, where he remained until October of the same year. From Boston he went to Saxonville, where he started in business. When his son, Alfred G. Priestly, was eight years old he was taken into his father's shop to learn the trade, and in 1870, at the death of his father, he took charge of the business, and has carried it on successfully ever since. When he first took possession the population of Saxonville numbered a few over one thousand inhabitants. It is now about twenty-five hundred. Mr. Priestly has watched his business increase from the time when he employed only five or six men until the present time. He now employs eighteen or twenty. He is Vice-President of the Master Painters' and Decorators' Association of Framingham, and strongly believes in coöperation for the betterment of the trade. The firm has always been in Saxonville, and has done work in Saxonville, Framingham, South Framingham and the neighboring villages.

Mr. W. H. Reddy of Framingham writes me:

"The oldest paint shop in Framingham, as far as I can find out, was established about 1820, by Messrs. Cloyes & Winter. They were between 1820 and 1860. Cloyes & Winter were partners for many years, having their place of business in the building near the corner of Pleasant and Vernon Streets. Mr. Winter came from Vermont and Mr. Cloyes was a native of Framingham.

"Then came George F. Ballard, for many years a master painter in Framingham. Ballard was also a native of Framingham.

"Then came George H. Graham and Frederick Coe, both from England. Coe came in 1847 and Graham in 1853. Mr. Graham was gifted for graining. Some of his work is to be seen today in Framingham. Then Mr. Graham's son, George H., Jr., succeeded him in business and carried it on for a number of years.

"At the same time, A. H. Stowell & Son were doing business and employing help. Graham & Son's place of business was in Central Square, halfway between Boston and Worcester, on the Old Turnpike Road, so called now, in a small attic in the house that they lived in. Stowell & Son's place of business was on Worcester Street.

"Then came C. P. Punchard, on Central Avenue, in the block that was burned about twenty-five years ago. He came from Boston and built a shop on the land on which my shop stands. He built my shop after the fire. Mr. Punchard did business for five or six years, then sold out to Charles A. Lynch, his foreman. Lynch did business for about two years and sold out to me in 1893. After the burning of the block that occupied the whole land between the two buildings (about 250 feet front), Punchard built my present shop.

GLOUCESTER

Albert Lane, Lanesville.

Mr. Lane started in the house painting business in 1857 and is still carrying it on, his shop being located in Lanesville, Mass.

HINGHAM

David Cobb & Son.

The shop now occupied by David Cobb & Son was first established by Seth B. Cushing as a paint store in 1832. He continued in business about six years, then gave up painting for other pursuits. David Cobb served four years' apprenticeship to Seth B. Cushing, 1834 to 1838, then hired a room in the next building for two years, when he bought the corner building of the row in 1840, and remained there until December, 1869, when he bought the present location, where he learned his trade. He took his two sons in partnership at that time. In 1880 one of his sons left and started for himself, and the firm name was changed to David Cobb & Son. It had always been David Cobb previous to 1880.

David Cobb, Sr., died December 15, 1909. He was ninety-two years old. His son, David, has been a member of the firm for over forty years and is now his successor in business.

HYDE PARK

A. W. Dunbar, rear 431 Hyde Park Avenue.

This shop was established by M. G. Dunbar in 1863. He was succeeded in 1871 by his son, A. W. Dunbar, who still conducts the business.

C. E. Palmer, 82 Fairmount Avenue.

C. E. Palmer, 82 Fairmount Avenue, has conducted a paint shop in Hyde Park for thirty-four years, since 1876. Mr. Palmer is a member of the Hyde Park Master Painters' Association.

LAWRENCE

James H. Clifford, 400 Essex Street.

Mr. Clifford has been in business in Lawrence nearly forty years.

W. A. Houston, 214 Broadway.

Mr. Houston took his first contract in 1869. Not having capital enough to run the business properly, he went to Boston the following year and worked one year. There was plenty of work at $3.00 per day. He returned the following year, a few hundred dollars ahead, and has carried on the business ever since.

Mr. Houston is a large dealer in paints, oils and varnishes, being a member of the Paint and Oil Club of New England. He is a past President of the Lawrence Association of Master Painters, and was President of the Society of Master House Painters and Decorators of Massachusetts in 1899, and is now serving on the Executive Board of the International Association of Master House Painters and Decorators.

Henry Morgan & Sons, 551 Haverhill Street.

In 1863 under the name of Morgan Brothers, Joseph H., William and Henry Morgan opened a paint shop in Pierce's Block on Broadway, Lawrence. After a few months they stored their traps in a room, gave up the shop, and enlisted in the army in Company B, Fourth Regiment, Massachusetts Volunteer Militia. William died in the service. After discharge, Joseph H. and Henry again opened shop under the name of Morgan Brothers, on the corner of Haverhill and Jackson Streets, where they were located for some time.

Mr. Henry Morgan went out of Lawrence to Cambridge and worked for J. H. & J. P. Thayer. Later he opened a shop on Third Street, East Cambridge, somewhere in the seventies, under the name of Tilden & Morgan. Mr. Tilden withdrew after a little while and Henry Morgan carried on the business in his own name.

Later he returned to Lawrence, opened a shop on Haverhill Street, near Broadway, and took his youngest brother with him, H. & E. Morgan being the firm name. Later Mr. E. Morgan sold out to Henry and removed to Sandford.

Henry Morgan then carried on business and later on took his sons into partnership, and still carries on business as Henry Morgan & Sons. Their shop is on Reservoir Street, Tower Hill.

The firm are members of the Lawrence Master Painters' Association.

LEXINGTON

Bailey Bros.

The business was founded by C. B. Bailey in 1872 and continued by him to October 3, 1877, at East Street. Since that time the business has been carried on by G. H. & E. C. Bailey, under the name of Bailey Bros. The firm are members of the Society of Master Painters and Decorators of Massachusetts.

LOWELL

Sylvester Bean, 316 Bridge Street.

Mr. Bean established himself in business at 316 Bridge Street in 1874, and has continued at the same stand ever since. He sells paints, oils, varnishes and small hardware in addition to conducting a general painting business.

P. A. Howard, 487 Merrimack Street.

H. B. Barnes had a paint shop on Merrimack Street, Lowell, about 1873. Mr. George S. Howard bought out the shop in 1893, and carried on the business for five years, when he retired. His brother, P. A. Howard, bought out the stock and has continued the business since that time at 487 Merrimack Street. He is a member of the Master Painters' Association.

Lowell Wall Paper Co., 97 Appleton Street.

George W. Chase started in the painting business in a small way in 1870. He did painting in connection with the carpenter's business. He started on Middlesex Street, and moved from there to Cushing Street, from there to Rock Street, and from there to Church Street, where he took on wall paper. He then moved to his present location at 97 Apple-ton Street, and employs from one to thirty men at different times. In 1891 he adopted the name "Lowell Wall Paper Company," to dis-tinguish it from his other business of carpenter and builder. At one time the firm was known as Livingstone & Chase. Mr. Chase is a member of the Master House Painters' and Decorators' Association.

Eugene N. Morrill, 36 Branch Street.

Nathaniel W. Morrill opened a paint and paper store on Gorham Street, Lowell, near the corner of Madison Street, in the year 1858.

In 1881 he removed his business to Middlesex Street, corner of Howard. where he continued in business until 1884, when ill health compelled him to retire from business, and his son, Eugene N., purchased the business, having been in his father's employ for a number of years previous to this time.

The business was continued at the old stand until 1904, when the shop was removed to its present location, at 33 Branch Street.

This is the oldest firm of its kind in this city at present, and one of the largest, if not the largest, paint and paper stores in Lowell, employ-ing from twelve to twenty-five men. Mr. Morrill is a member of the Lowell Master Painters' Association.

LYNN.

William L. Baird, 17 Centre Street.

The business was established in 1850 by William Baird and Merrill Walden, as Baird & Walden. Their first location was on Sight Street; later they removed to Western Avenue, opposite Sight Street, and next to Western Avenue, corner Centre Street, when Mr. Walden left the firm to go to Memphis, Tenn. The business was continued by William Baird, who afterward removed to South Common Street, next to the Universalist Church, then to the Arcade, Market Square, as William

Baird & Son, from there to the present location on Centre Street, corner Western Avenue.

William Baird died in 1884, and the business was continued by William L. Baird and Robert E. Redman, as William L. Baird & Co., until 1897, when Mr. Redman left the firm. The business has since been carried on by William L. Baird.

In this time the various firms have always paid one hundred cents on the dollar, and were the first painters in this city to establish weekly payments of wages, in 1864, since which time they have never failed to pay wages in full on Saturday.

At the outbreak of the War of the Rebellion in 1861, Mr. Baird enlisted and served through the war. Returning home he succeeded to his father in business, and later was elected Mayor of the city of Lynn. He is a member of the Society of Master House Painters and Decorators of Massachusetts.

Stephen Sullivan, 6 Sutton Street.

Daniel Sullivan opened a paint shop in Lynn about 1868, and was succeeded by a nephew, Stephen Sullivan, who conducts a shop at 6 Sutton Street.

MALDEN

C. P. Hicks & Co., 417–421 Main Street.

This shop was established about 1859 by a man named Greene. The present proprietors have been in possession about fifteen years.

Frederick M. Noyes, 116 Main Street.

Frederick M. Noyes started in business in Boston in 1870, moving to Malden in 1872, where he has continued to the present time.

H. N. Perrigo, 1 Bird Court.

Mr. H. N. Perrigo has been in the painting business in Malden since 1873, located in various places. His present place of business has been 1 Bird Court, which he has occupied for the last ten years.

MARBLEHEAD

Carvill & Shattuck.

The business of Carvill & Shattuck was established about 1880, and is still continued by the original partners.

L. C. Harrison.

The business was established about 1871 by W. R. Arrington, and passed in 1909 to L. C. Harrison, the present proprietor.

J. S. Wormstead, 11 State Street.

The business was established in 1843. At the death of the founder in 1888, it descended to his son, Mr. J. S. Wormstead, the present proprietor. There have been no other changes.

MEDFORD

Warren H. Keay, 40 High Street.

This shop was established by Edward Poor in March, 1874. He was succeeded by Dawson & Porter in August, 1888. Mr. Porter retired a few years later, and the business was conducted by C. E. Dawson.

In February, 1899, Fitzgerald & Keay purchased the business, and in June, 1901, Warren H. Keay bought out his partner and has conducted the business to this date. The shop has remained in the same location since its establishment, except one change across the street.

MIDDLEBORO

H. A. Sparrow, Rock Street.

Mr. Sparrow and Mr. G. H. Shaw, under the firm name of Shaw & Sparrow, opened a paint shop in Middleboro, Mass., in 1852. Mr. Sparrow retired from the firm two years later, and conducted a business in his own name until 1860, when he formed a partnership with Mr. C. H. Rogers, under the name of Rogers & Sparrow. This firm continued until 1864, when both enlisted in the army. Mr. Sparrow being discharged, soon afterward returned to the painting business, which he has conducted in his own name until the present time.

NAHANT

J. Colby Wilson, Nahant and Pride's Crossing, Mass.

The firm was established in 1868 as Rowell & Wilson, doing business in Lynn and Nahant. In 1871 this firm divided, Mr. Rowell continuing the Lynn business, and J. Colby Wilson the Nahant end. Mr. Wilson has continued the business at Nahant until now, under his name. In 1898 his son, H. C. Wilson, came into the firm, and in 1899 they opened a branch store at Pride's Crossing, Beverly, and have continued it since, doing work all along the North Shore from Gloucester to Nahant. Mr. Rowell has been dead for some years.

NANTUCKET

H. Paddack & Co., established about 1775.

Abisha Paddack, born in Nantucket, 1754, carried on the business of house and ship painting in his very early manhood. He was succeeded by his sons, Seth, Laban, John and Hezekiah, later by grandsons, Frederick, David, George, and by others, collateral members of the family.

It can safely be said that for over one hundred and thirty-five years the family name of Paddack has been intimately connected with the painting business in the town of Nantucket, and no doubt exists that the first regular shop was established by Abisha Paddack.

During all the intervening years the location of the business has not been outside a stone's throw of the building now owned and occupied by the firm of H. Paddack & Co., at the corner of Main and Washington Streets.

Mr. Henry Paddack retired from the firm about 1890, and the present members of the firm are E. G. Thomas and H. B. Smith.

NEW BEDFORD

F. T. Akin & Co., 9 North Water Street.

Mr. Francis T. Akin started in the painting and decorating business at 13 Rodman Street, January 12, 1860. He remained at that location until September 20, 1872, when he moved into the shop now occupied by F. T. Akin & Company, 9 North Water Street. Mr. Akin will have conducted the paint business fifty years on Januray 12, 1910.

This firm are also large dealers in paints, oil and varnishes.

Mr. Thomas B. Akin directs and supervises the practical work done by the firm. He is an ex-President of the New Bedford Master Painters' Association, and an ex-President of the Society of Master House Painters and Decorators of Massachusetts.

William T. Caswell, 34 Union Street.

This business was established by W. H. Caswell previous to 1850. His son and grandson are partners in the business. The senior member of the firm is still alive and hearty. They are members of the Master Painters' Association.

T. J. Moriarty, 184 Fourth Street.

Joseph T. Moriarty served his apprenticeship with Francis T. Akin, which culminated in 1874. He, however, remained in the same employ until three years later, when he established himself in business at 533 South Water Street, where he continued with his brother, the present incumbent, who joined him in 1885, until May, 1889, when they removed to the present establishment at 184 Fourth Street, adding a line of wall paper, moulding, etc.

In 1893, in the month of February, Joseph T. retired to assume the sale of Geo. Kirby, Jr. & Co.'s paint products in New York and the eastern States, remaining with that firm until five years ago, when he withdrew from the paint business entirely, and began the manufacture of shoe laces and similar goods, locating in Philadelphia.

Mr. T. J. Moriarty, continuing the shop at the same location with good success, added in 1904 a comprehensive line of hardware, which venture proved very successful. With Mr. Moriarty is associated his son, who has known no other occupation since leaving school, sixteen years ago.

The firm are members of the New Bedford Master Painters' Association.

William R. West, 830 Purchase Street.

The business was established by Mr. William R. West, in 1879, at 838 Purchase Street. Later he removed to 830 Purchase Street, where he still carries on business.

Mr. West conducts a large store for the sale of painters' and decorators' materials, and is a member of the local Master Painters' Association.

NEWBURYPORT

F. E. Cutter & Son.

F. E. Cutter & Son were for over thirty years in business on Mechanic Street, Newburyport. The firm has now retired from business, owing to the illness of the senior member.

Green Davis, 37 and 41 State Street.

Mr. Green Davis writes me as follows:

"The business was established in August, 1871, in a shop on Unicorn Street, for many years occupied by George Cutter, a skilled coach and carriage painter, who painted all the stagecoaches used by the Eastern Stage Company in those days in this vicinity.

"I remained there less than a year, and finding it too small to accommodate my increasing business, removed to 10 Green Street, another old carriage painting shop, where I remained for several years. I then leased for a term of fifteen years the large brick building at the foot of Green Street on Merrimac, Nos. 38 and 40, a building that was 45 x 35, three stories and basement. Like the two previous establishments, the building had been for generations occupied by the house painters and decorators.

"At this stand, in addition to the stock previously carried of paint supplies, doors, windows, blinds, and frames, I added the largest and best wall paper department to be found outside of Boston, but here also before my lease expired my increasing business demanded better location and more convenient methods, and I bought the three-story brick block corner of State and Essex Streets, containing three large stores, two of which I have fitted up for my business, including the basement of the three stores, and in addition leasing and occupying two stories of a wooden building in the rear of same, about 30 x 50 feet.

"Since locating here I have added several new departments to the business, and my workshop is in the wooden building, thus separating it from the store business. I still continue to do, as in the beginning, nothing but first-class work, but find it more difficult to get good all-around workmen each year."

NEWTON

Bemis & Jewett, Newton Centre.

The firm of Bemis & Jewett was established at Newton Centre previous to 1880. They have another shop at Needham and do a large business. The firm is a member of the Master Painters' Association.

J. M. Briggs & Son, 322 Washington Street.

Mr. J. M. Briggs started business in Newton in 1869. His place of business for the past thirty-three years has been at 322 Washington Street.

Mr. Briggs' son, Frank H. Briggs, has been in his father's employ for the past fifteen years, and the firm name was changed to J. M. Briggs & Son about twelve years ago.

J. W. Conroy & Son, West Newton.

This shop was established by J. W. Conroy in 1875, who located at 19 Chestnut Street, and the shop remained in the same location until 1908, when it had to be vacated to make room for a new building.

In 1880 Mr. Conroy took his son, Eugene F., into partnership as J. W. Conroy & Son.

J. W. Conroy died in 1889, and his son has continued the business since that time, using the old firm name.

R. F. Cranitch, Walnut Street, Newtonville.

This shop was established by John O. Evans about 1840, on the corner of Washington and Walnut Streets, about where the bridge is now. Later it changed hands as follows: M. T. Haywood, Cranitch & Horrigan, L. H. Cranitch, and R. F. Cranitch.

L. H. Cranitch moved the shop to 250 Walnut Street, the present location, about 1885. Mr. Cranitch is a member of the Master Painters' Association.

George S. Noden, 22 Nonantum Place.

The business was established in May, 1881, under the firm name of Noden & Smith, and continued as such until May, 1882, when the copartnership was dissolved, and Mr. George S. Noden has since carried on the business under his own name.

Mr. Noden is a member of the Master Painters' Association.

PITTSFIELD

Bryan O'Laughlin, 31 North Street.

Bryan O'Laughlin has carried on the painting business in Pittsfield for over forty years.

PLYMOUTH

L. C. Howland & Son, 13 Middle Street.

The firm of L. C. Howland & Son was established in 1859 by Mr. Lemuel C. Howland, who located on Sandwich Street, Plymouth. The business growing rapidly, it was removed to Middle Street in 1884. In 1897 Mr. Howland's son, Mr. Herbert Howland, was taken into the firm under the name of L. C. Howland & Son. The founder of the firm died in 1902, and the business is now carried on by the son, Mr. Herbert Howland, at the same address and under the same name.

PROVINCETOWN

B. H. Dyer & Co.

The business was established by B. H. Dyer in 1853 at Truro, Mass., and in May, 1865, Mr. Dyer moved to Provincetown, opening a shop a few doors east of their present location. The present shop was built in 1867. In 1880 a hardware and building material department was opened, under the name of B. H. Dyer & Co., and in 1887 the whole business was united under the same firm name, and has so continued until the present time. Mr. Dyer was the sole proprietor up to July of 1907, when he transferred the business to his wife and daughter, who now own it. Mr. Dyer died in October, 1907. Since 1880, Mr. George F. Miller has been in charge of the sales and store work, and is now conducting the business. They are the oldest paint concern at that end of the Cape.

SALEM

John B. Chamberlain, 18 Bickford Street.

Jim and Sam Ferguson were master painters in Salem about 1850, going out of the business in the late sixties.

John B. Chamberlain, 18 Bickford Street, is their successor.

Harlow & Baker, 3 Walnut Street.

Daniel Henderson, whose paint shop was on Walnut Street, succeeded to the business established by his father between 1810 and 1820. This shop is now conducted by Harlow & Baker at 3 Walnut Street.

J. C. Martin, rear of 10 Dodge Street.

About 1830 G. A. Pousland carried on a painting business at 29 Peabody Street, Salem. In 1837 the business was moved to 18 Peabody Street, and was conducted under the name of Rhodes & Pousland. About 1850 the partnership was dissolved, and G. A. Pousland conducted the business until 1865. At that date, J. C. Martin went into business with G. A. Pousland, and continued until Mr. Pousland's death in 1897. Since that time the business has been carried on by J. C. Martin, first at 16 Peabody Street, and now located at rear 10 Dodge Street.

John P. Monaghan, North Street.

John P. Monaghan established a paint shop on North Street, Salem, in 1868, and has remained in practically the same location until 1910. Mr. Monaghan writes me that all the old painters of Salem had no fires or failures, and in consequence they have little money.

S. S. Symonds & Co., 1 Franklin Street.

The business was established in 1847 by S. S. Symonds, at what was then 79 North Street, where he remained until in the '70's, when he moved to the building next south, using that and a room of the next building for some years, until about 1890, when he moved to his present location, 1 Franklin Street. In 1882 his son, also S. S. Symonds, was admitted to partnership, and the business was conducted under the name of S. S. Symonds & Co., until the death of the elder Mr. Symonds, in June, 1902, when the son succeeded to the business, and is still carrying it on under the same firm name.

SOMERVILLE

W. J. Fermoyle, 250 Pearl Street, Somerville.

F. W. Johnson established a paint shop on Medford Street, Somerville, about 1860, and continued in business until 1894, when two of his employees, W. J. Fermoyle and Frank Butler, purchased the business. Six years later Mr. Butler withdrew from the firm, and since that time Mr. W. J. Fermoyle has conducted the business. In 1887 the building was moved from Medford Street to the present location. Mr. Fermoyle is a member of the Somerville Master Painters' Association.

Benjamin R. Twombly, 16½ Union Square.

Mr. J. Q. Twombly opened a paint shop in the town of Somerville, Mass., in 1846, locating close to what is now Union Square. At that time the population was less than three thousand, and so far as I can learn this was the first shop located in the town.

Mr. Twombly continued actively in business until his death in 1902, and was succeeded by his son, Benj. R. Twombly, who for twenty years previous had been in his father's employ.

A shop was built on Milk Street (now Somerville Avenue), close to Union Square, in 1867. About 1890 this shop was removed to 32 Bennett Street, where it still stands. Mr. B. R. Twombly is a past President of the Somerville Master Painters' Association.

George H. Wickes & Son, 54 Broadway.

M. J. Goodwin established a paint shop at rear of 54 Broadway, Somerville, about 1877, and continued in business until about 1900, when he sold out to George H. Wickes & Son. George H. Wickes had formerly been a partner with Thomas Anderson of Somerville, under the name of Anderson & Wickes, from 1879. At the death of Mr. Anderson, Mr. Wickes continued the business, and admitted his son to partnership.

SPRINGFIELD

T. W. Gilbert, 134–136 State Street.

Mr. Gilbert started in business as a house painter and decorator in 1870. His first shop was at 449 State Street. Five years later he removed his shop to 134–136 State Street, and has remained in that location over twenty-five years. Some of his employees have been with him ever since he began business.

Albert Hancox Co., corner Barnes and Bridge Streets.

This business was founded by Albert Hancox over thirty years ago. Mr. Hancox died several years ago. The shop is now conducted for the heirs by Mr. Sullivan.

The Old Corner Decorating Co., 66 Bridge Street.

This business was originally established in 1834, and was known as the Old Corner Bookstore. They carried a stock of books and wall paper, and it later was operated by Messrs. Whitney & Adams. The present firm has been established for ten years under the firm name, but dates its beginning to the Old Corner Bookstore.

The business is incorporated with the following gentlemen as its officers: F. W. Havens, President; W. H. Strout, Secretary; S. D. Church, Treasurer and Manager.

STONEHAM

E. F. Saurin, 26 Central Street.

Mr. Saurin began business in Stoneham, January 1, 1861, at the corner of Main and Hersam Streets. In 1869 he built a shop at 17 Franklin Street, and remained there until 1889, when the premises were sold. He then bought a lot and erected a building known as "Saurin Block," where his shop was located until November 15, 1906. He then moved his shop to 26 Central Street, where it still remains.

Mr. Saurin is known as an expert grainer, and is now in his seventy-fifth year.

STOUGHTON

C. A. Howland.

Mr. C. A. Howland of Stoughton writes me as follows:

"My father, Calvin Howland, was carrying on the painting business under the name of C. Howland, in Stoughton, when I was born. That was March 6, 1843. How much before that I can't remember. He continued in the business until he died, November 8, 1883.

"After the war, where I served two enlistments, I went to work for him, about 1865. In 1874 I went into partnership with him, under the firm name of C. Howland & Son. He was killed by a fall November 8, 1883. After that I kept the shop going just the same, to the present time, under the name of C. A. Howland. It is safe to say that our shop has run seventy, possibly seventy-five years, with no other change. I do not know of any shop that was started before that time.

"As there is no one to take my place, the shop will stop when I do, but I am all right. I have made a business of steeple painting for almost fifty years, and I still do all the high work myself. I take all the contracts I get, and do that kind of work for other painters who can't very well do the high work themselves.

"I hope this information will not come too late to help you in your paper. If you think of anything you would like to know, write and I will answer by return mail."

Mr. Howland painted the steeple of the Park Street Church, Boston, about twenty years ago, and has made a specialty of that kind of work for nearly fifty years.

TAUNTON

H. L. Davis Co.

Mr. H. L. Davis established a paint shop and wall-paper store on Broadway, Taunton, in the year 1876, employing about twelve men during the busy season. In 1877 he removed to 34 Main Street, and started the framing of pictures in addition to his other business. At this time the total of the year's business was about twelve thousand dollars. The business continued to grow and prosper, and in 1887 Mr. E. W. Sturgis became a partner. Mr. Sturgis started as a clerk with Mr. Davis when the store was located on Broadway, and has been with and a part of the H. L. Davis Company continuously ever since.

Shortly after Mr. Sturgis became a partner, window shades, draperies and an art gallery were added to the establishment.

In 1890 they removed to larger quarters at 36 Main Street, where they occupy a four-story brick building, using all the floor and basement as stock and sales rooms. They occupy besides a near-by building as a paint shop, and have two rooms in the next building as drapery workrooms and stockrooms.

In February, 1900, Mr. H. L. Davis died, and in January, 1901, the business was incorporated under the laws of Massachusetts, Mr. E. W. Sturgis being chosen President, Mr. I. H. Bosworth, Treasurer, and Mr. A. C. Lewis, Secretary; Mr. Davis' widow still retaining an interest in the business.

The force now comprises thirty painters and paper-hangers, and twelve men in the sales departments, and the business aggregates about sixty thousand dollars a year. They have recently remodeled the entire interior of the store, and at the present time have one of the most up-to-date decorative departments in New England.

C. Wood & Son, 65 Main Street.

The painting, decorating and paper-hanging firm of C. Wood & Son, located at 65 Main Street, is the oldest established in the city, dating back sixty years, and has a reputation for reliability and excellence of service. The business was founded by Cornelius Wood, who located in Taunton in 1850, coming from London, England, with others at that time. Mr. Wood worked with his brother-in-law, James Darke, a couple of years, after which he brought out the business, and continued the same in Crandell's Block, on Weir Street, until the great fire in 1855, which devastated the greater part of the business section of the city. Being forced to find a new shop, he located on School Street, remaining there but a short time, only to move his shop to Main Street, in the building now occupied by T. C. Baker. From here he moved his place of business to Gilmore's store on the corner of Main and Trescott Streets, adding a line of paper hangings at this time. He was soon forced to move again on account of a fire, which did great damage to his stock of paper. After Gilmore's Block was built in 1871, he made it his place of business until 1879, when he purchased the property at 65 Main Street, and after extensive alterations and a large addition, he moved into his new store and has been doing business there ever since. At this time he took his son, William H. Wood, into partnership with him.

Mr. Cornelius Wood is the oldest business man on the street, and may be seen almost daily at the store, still being interested in the business, although in the fall of 1908 he deeded over his interest in the concern to his grandson, Louis T. Wood, who with his father carries on the business.

WALTHAM

Charles A. Poole, 7 Elm Street.

This shop was established in 1839 by E. M. Hutchinson, who conducted it for thirty-seven years. In 1876 Lane & Poole were his successors. Mr. Lane retired in 1886, since which time Mr. C. A. Poole has been sole proprietor and can be found at his shop daily.

B. W. Wentworth & Son, 3 Prospect Street.

Mr. B. W. Wentworth established a paint shop on Main Street, near Lexington Street, Waltham, in 1858. About 1880 the shop was moved to 3 Prospect Street, where it still remains. In 1888 his son, Mr. John E. Wentworth, was taken into partnership and the firm name changed to B. W. Wentworth & Son. Mr. B. W. Wentworth has been dead several years, but the business is still conducted by his son as B. W. Wentworth & Son.

WATERTOWN

George A. Page, Merchants Row.

The painting firm of Page was established in Watertown in the year 1835 by Harrison P. Page. On his retirement in 1859 he was succeeded by his brother, John, who had previously been in his employ, and who carried on the business until 1889, when he was succeeded by his son, George A. Page, the present proprietor.

WESTFORD

Joe Wall, Graniteville, Westford, Mass.

Joe Wall and his brother began business in 1889. In 1899 they bought from the heirs the stock and tools of Jonas Butterfield, whose shop was established in 1850, and this became his successor in business.

WOBURN

Robert H. Magee, 11 Bennett Street.

The business was established by John G. Cole in 1840, who was succeeded by Matthews & Layton. In 1881 Robert H. Magee succeeded to the business and still carries it on at 877A Main Street.

WORCESTER

A. & W. Ballou, rear of 12 Pleasant Street.

In 1848 Amasa Ballou established himself as a master painter and decorator in Worcester, Mass. In 1852 he admitted Marshall Drury to partnership, the firm being Ballou & Drury. Their shop was at the corner of Norwich and Mechanic Streets, and later on Maple Street. In 1854 Mr. Drury retired and Amasa Ballou conducted the business in his own name. In the early sixties he moved his shop to the rear of 10 Pleasant Street, and in 1894 his son, Walter F., was admitted to partnership. The firm is still actively engaged in painting and decorating, although the senior partner is unable to give the business his personal attention, as in former years.

F. W. Estabrook, rear 49 Main Street.

The firm was established by the senior Mr. Estabrook about 1870. His son succeeded him about 1890.

L. B. Holt, 626 Main Street.

R. H. Chase established a paint shop in Worcester previous to 1870, and on his death the business was purchased by L. B. Holt, who still conducts the shop.

Stenberg & Co., 390 Main Street.

Philip A. Butler was one of the pioneer church decorators in New England, who in the year 1848 established himself in business in Boston, and continued to do decorative painting until the early seventies, when G. L. Stenberg, a graduate from the firm of Haberstroh & Needham, was taken into partnership, the firm being Butler & Stenberg, located at 17 Pemberton Square, Boston. Mr. Butler retired from business in 1886, and G. L. Stenberg and F. A. Stenberg continued the business under the name of Stenberg & Co. at 5 Tremont Place and later removed to Worcester, making that city the headquarters of the firm.

It will be noticed that the oldest shop in Massachusetts, in continuous existence, is that of H. Paddack & Co., of Nantucket, which was established in 1775.

The next oldest shop operated by one family is that of J. H. & J. P. Thayer & Co., of Cambridge, established in 1790.

The oldest shop in Boston is that of D. E. Bryan, established by C. H. Knox, 1831; the next oldest, that of Charles Cabot, established by Henry Cabot in 1833; the next oldest, John Cotton & Son, established by Jacob Thaxter in 1834.

The oldest shop under one management is that of George Williams & Son, established in 1845.

Before closing it might be well to consider briefly the changes in the appearance of the average paint shop in the last fifty years.

During that time there has been a radical change in the administration of the business. A cellar or old stable is no longer considered an ideal location for a paint shop. Many of the larger firms of painters and decorators have elegant offices adorned with pictures, bronzes, rugs, etc.; the price of any one of these things would be sufficient to furnish half a dozen offices of the master painters of two or more generations ago.

The master painter of fifty or more years ago relied for decorative effect on the practical work of his own hands, and the walls of his office (when he had one) were adorned chiefly by panels, showing his ability in decorative art, graining, marbling, etc. In this respect he was the superior of the average master painter of today, for the most successful painters of today are, as a rule, better versed in the business side of the trade than in the practical execution of decorative art.

It cannot be gainsaid that the master painters' associations have been an important factor in causing the improved surroundings of the office and shop. The fact that the progressive men in the trade travel more than formerly, and are more observant, quick to appropriate ideas and adapt them to their several localities, is a reason for much of the improvement we see in offices and shops.

The Master Painters of Massachusetts affiliated with the International Association have from the first been identified with the movement for the betterment of the craft, and have sent representatives or delegates to every convention of the parent body, beginning with the first convention at Chicago in 1885. In visiting the various large cities of the country, the Association Master Painter is given opportunities for seeing decorative art which are denied to the casual visitor. His brothers of the brush see to it that the finest examples of work in their city are brought to his attention.

Some of the most enduring friendships are formed between members of the craft at these annual gatherings, which furnish an opportunity to talk over old times and discuss the problems that daily confront the master painter.

Brother Farwell J. Thayer of the Cambridge Association, referring to the death of Ex-President William F. Gilbert, writes me as follows:

"These men are fast dropping off, and as I look at the picture of the Association members, it is with a sense of sadness and longing, and with gladness, too, as I think of the good qualities in each one of them. I also feel glad that I have known them and labored with them. How we shall miss Brother Gilbert! his admirable qualities of heart and head endeared him to us, and we shall feel lonely without him. Upright and honorable in all his dealings, he lived up to all his agreements; a good fellow, a good friend and good business man, careful and circumspect.

"He had that same stern integrity and native manliness which characterized Brother William B. Holt, and he was loyal to our organization and all its members. Truly a good man has gone.

"If our organization was successful in nothing else, it *did* break down barriers between competitors, creating, instead, lasting friendships, and as we look back, we recognize in each of our departed brothers many things to admire and respect, and it makes us glad we have known them and worked with them."

GRAINING
ANCIENT and MODERN

❡ The most complete and profusely illustrated book on graining ever published

55 Colored Illustrations. Price $3.00

SEND STAMP FOR SAMPLE ILLUSTRATION

WRITTEN AND PUBLISHED BY
WILLIAM E. WALL, SOMERVILLE, MASS.